the native foods restaurant cookbook

the
native foods
restaurant
cookbook

Tanya Petrovna

foreword by
DEBORAH MADISON

illustrations by
STEPHEN BROGDON

SHAMBHALA

BOSTON & LONDON 2003

Shambhala Publications, Inc.
Horticultural Hall
300 Massachusetts Avenue
Boston, Massachusetts 02115
www.shambhala.com

9 8 7 6 5 4 3 2 1

First Edition

Printed in the United States of America

∞ This edition is printed on acid-free paper that meets the
American National Standards Institute z39.48 Standard.

Distributed in the United States by Random House, Inc.,
and in Canada by Random House of Canada Ltd

Interior design and composition: Greta D. Sibley & Associates

Library of Congress Cataloging-in-Publication Data
Petrovna, Tanya, 1960–
The Native Foods restaurant cookbook / Tanya Petrovna.—1st ed.
p.   cm.
Includes index.
ISBN 1-59030-076-9 (pbk.: alk. paper)
1. Vegetarian cookery. I. Native Foods (Restaurant) II. Title.
TX837.P5137 2003
641.5'636—dc21
2003007003

Food Incantation

With feet grounded
Place hands palm down above food

Mother Goddess,
Father God
thank you for Earth;
beautiful, precious planet on which I live.
Grateful now I receive this gift;
delicious, nourishing gift of food
from the bounty of the Earth.
For my body's use
I take in with ease the full power of this food,
then joyfully, elegantly, I give back to the earth
that which I do not need.
I blend myself with All that Is.
So be it
and
so it is.

—Mathu Zephyr

contents

Food Incantation   v

Foreword by Deborah Madison   xvii

Acknowledgments   xxi

Introduction   1

Native Foods and Me   2
The Vegetarian Lifestyle   7
Passionate about Organics   12

part one   *The Basics*

The Setup   17

Know Your Ingredients: A Glossary of Foods   17
The Well-Equipped Kitchen: A Glossary
        of Utensils   32
Preparation and Cooking   37
    A Glossary of Cooking Terms   37
    La Technique: A Glossary of Preparation and
        Cooking Methods   44
Measure for Measure   49

Basic Beanery   51

Know Your Beans   51
How to Cook Beans   55

Grains for Brains   57
    Basic Grain Cookery   61

Tempeh: Food of the Gods
  and Goddesses   63
    Tempeh Basic Prep   65
    Simple Deglaze   65

Seitan: The Protein of Wheat   66
    Makin' Seitan   69
    Seitan Broth   70

Soy Protein Textures: Whaddaya Mean
  It's Not Meat?   72
    Reconstitution for Granules, Bits, or Flakes   74
    Taco Meat   74
    Italian Ground Around   75
    Reconstitution for Soy Chunks   75
    Reconstitution for Soy Brests   76
    Basic Marinade   76
    Sautéed and Grilled Brests   77

How Do You Do Tofu?   78
    Basic Tofu Marinade   80

part two   *The Recipes*

Complement with Condiments   85
    Roasted Garlic Cloves   86
    Garlic Toast   87

Toasted Almond and Currant Chutney   88

Cucumber Quick Pickles   89

Pretty Pink Pickles   90

Curried Cashew Crunch   91

Country Croutons   92

Cranberry Orange Relish   93

Toasted Sesame Seeds   94

Gomasio (Sesame Salt)   95

Miso Lemon Carrottops   96

Native Ch'i's (Nondairy Cheese)   97

Tofu Ricotta   98

Tofu Feta   99

Salsa de Chupacabra   100

Ray's Good Home Blackening Spice   101

Caramelized Onions   102

Get Dressed!   103

Basic Balsamic Vinaigrette   104

Green Goddess   105

Greek Lemon Garlic Dressing   106

Mango Lime Vinaigrette   107

Pumpkin Plum Dressing   108

Ponzu (Japanese Soy Citrus Dressing)   109

Sesame Orange Vinaigrette   110

Thousand Island Dressing   111

Caesar's Vegan   112

Black Creek Ranch Dressing   113

Curry Lime Vinaigrette   114

Madison's Garden Dressing   115

Get Sauced!   116

Gandhi's Curry Sauce   117

Simple Marinara   118

Baja Enchilada   119
Italian Salsa   120
Salsa Fresca   121
Thai Peanut Sauce   122
Pumpkin Seed Pesto   123
Creamy Wild Mushroom   124
Shallot Mushroom Gravy   125
Sassy Sweet and Sour Sauce   126
Green Tea Sesame Sauce   127
Bessie's (Thank-You) BBQ Sauce   128
Tartar Sauce   129
Jamaican Jerk Marinade   130
Flamed Banana Salsa   131
Rockin' Moroccan Marinade   132
Hollandaise Sauce   133

Snacks 'n' Apps   134

Edamame (Sweet Green Soybeans)   135
Harry's Hummus   136
Ruth's Awesome Threesome   137
Tempeh Pâté   138
French Love Bites   139
Tata's Tapenade   140
Spanakopita   141
Zen Cucumber Bites   143
Papa's Yugoslavian Ivar   144
Sophie's Stuffed Mushrooms   145
Cauliflower Crudité with Sesame Curry Dip   146
Guacamole   147
Speedy Kim Chee   148
Native Nachos   149
Thai Sticks   150

Soup of the Day 151

Mighty Miso 152
Russian Velvet 153
Loving Lentil 154
Nacho Gazpacho 155
Atomic Split Pea 156
Caldo Verde (Portuguese Greens Soup) 157
Cravin' Corn Chowder 158
Black Bean Soup with Masa Balls 159
Whirled Peas 161
Fresh Asparagus Soup 162
Butternut Squash and Lemon Grass Bisque 163
Manilow's Minestrone 164

Salads 166

Mecca Azteca Salad 167
Warm and Wild Mushroom Salad 168
California Caesar 169
Soy Amigo 170
Tanya's Tempeh Salad 171
Simple Pleasures 172
José y Jesus' Jicama Salad 173
Iron Yam 174
Native Chop Chop 175
Bye Bye Barnum Black Bean Salad 176
Perestroika (Russian Salad) 177
Quick Tofu Egg 178
Chinese "Save the Chicken" Salad 179
Fellini's Dream 180
Gorgeous Greek 181
Farrah's Fattoush 182
Fleetwood Macaroni Salad 183

Lemon Potato Salad   184
Wheat Berry Waldorf Salad   185
Watermelon Chill   186
TuNO   187
Thai Slaw   188
Quinoa Tabouli   189

Sandwiches, Wraps, and Burritos   190

'70s Delight   191
TuNO Salad Sandwich   192
Hot Italian   193
Philly Peppersteak   194
Palm Springs Wrap (Tempeh Salad Wrap)   196
California Caesar Wrap with Tempeh   197
Bali Surf Burger   198
Ciao Bella Burger   199
Rocket Burger   200
Poltz Burrito   201
El Bruncho Burrito   202
Zucchini Rosemary Sandwich   203
BBQ Love Burger   204
Tijuana Tacos   205
Korean Tacos   206
Tuesday's Mediterranean Sandwich   207
Bagel No Lox   209
Bagel E   210

Entrées   211

Totally Stacked Enchiladas   212
Gandhi Bowl   214
Tempeh Scaloppine with Shallot
        Mushroom Gravy   215

Tempeh Provençale   216

Hungarian Goulash   217

Oopa Moussaka   218

Stroganoff Seitansky   220

Seitan Olé Molé   221

Tofu Short Stack   223

Le Benedict Florentine   224

Fun Mung Curry   225

Mad Cowboy   227

Eggplant Rollatini   229

Chicken Fried Steak   230

Flaming Fajitas   231

Steak Morocco   232

Thai Tempeh Stir-Fry   233

Good Karma Sarma: Cabbage Rolls   234

The Hollywood Bowl   236

Sweet and Sour Nuggets   237

Puff Pastry Pot Pies   238

Pasta Bolognese   240

Rasta Pasta Primavera   241

Jerked "Save the Chicken"   242

Side Dishes   243

Kissed French Toast   244

Tofu Scrambler   245

In Thyme for Breakfast Potatoes   246

Cranberry Chestnut Stuffing   247

Roasted Winter Roots and Vegetables   248

Sautéed Chard with Onions   249

Tzimmes   250

Steamed Artichokes   251

Coconut Groove Rice   253

Vera's Voluptuous Veggie Fried Rice   254

Japanese Fried Rice   255

Mama's Mexican Rice   256

Love Potion Green Beans   257

Roasted Garlic Mashed Potatoes   258

Get Yo' Greens   259

Roasted Lemon Potatoes   260

Tangerine Yams   261

Tequila Lime Yams   262

Leek 'n' Lemon   263

Kasha Varnishkas   264

Fred's Corn Bread   265

East Indian Onion Bread (Naan)   266

Won't You Arame, Bill   267

Hijiki à la Tanji   268

Neato Refritos: Mexican Refried Beans   269

Summer Grilled Vegetables   270

Sweet Treats   271

Carrot Cake with Dream Cheese Frosting   272

Key Lime Parfait   274

Chai Pumpkin Pie   275

Mr. Weld's Banana Cream Pie   276

Flaky Pie Crust   277

Tastes Like Caramel Apple   278

Elephant Chocolate Cake   279

Quickie Banana Almond Sundae   281

Martha's Glazed Nuts   282

Chocolate French Silk Lingerie Pie   283

Sam's Vegan Cheesecake   285

Lulu's Lemon Cake   286

Pineapple Upside Down Cake   288

Chocolate Mint Holiday Balls   290
Chocolate Cherry Cookies   291
Jungle Boogie Bars   292
Gertrude's Ya-Ya Apple Strudel   293
Eleni's California Baklava   295
Juan's Flan   297
Apple Pudding   298
Japanese Jiggy Jell   299
Chestnut Yam Pudding Cream   300
Vanilla Crème   301
Sambuca Crème   302
Sweet Ginger Cream   303

Specialty Drinks   304

Native Iced Tea   305
Mexican Hot Chocolate   306
Guru Chai   307
Palm Desert Date Shake   308
El Choco-Banana   309
Crystal Blue Persuasion   310
Lavender Lemonade   311
Mocha Frappé   312
Cranberry Shrub   313
Roasted Barley Tea   314

In Closing   315

Index   317

foreword

I first met Tanya Petrovna at a conference on the vegetarian food guide pyramid that was put on by Oldways Preservation and Trust several years ago. I was intrigued by the name on her card, "Native Foods," thinking that it was about Native American cooking, which it isn't, as it turns out. But I was also intrigued by Tanya herself, by her enormous enthusiasm and very real warmth.

A year later and a few days before Christmas, my husband and I were in Palm Springs. After a long day of travel, we had arrived too late for dinner with his family, but I remembered Tanya's restaurant. I even had her card, which was amazing in itself, so we set out for a pre-Christmas vegan dinner. Tanya was in command, and she took good care of us, making sure we had one of her tempeh dishes and that we ended with a vegan chocolate cake. The food was delicious and we felt good eating it. I was a bit skeptical, but with her commitment to good ingredients and skill in the kitchen, Tanya succeeded in making wholesome food that was a pleasure to eat. If her restaurant were in my neighborhood, I'd probably drop in a few times a week. It's the kind of food you know you can live well on.

Tanya's book is a generous invitation to your success. And while she doesn't say that this is a book for a beginning cook, there's plenty of introductory material that kindly takes a new cook into account. For those who perhaps haven't yet set up a kitchen, there's a helpful guide to doing just that. For those whose vocabulary of basic cooking terms and preparation methods is scant, a glossary appears. How considerate!

Products like tempeh, which tend to get relegated to vegan-land where no one but a dedicated few finds them, are explained. There's a great glossary of foods that has the kind of mix that suggests an open mind: balsamic vinegar and barley malt syrup. Coconut milk and gluten flour. Hijiki and lavosh. Her sugar is organic, but it's sugar, and that means that foods cooked with it will be familiar, not weird dishes whose names are the only familiar part, and that's important if people are to branch out of their known territories. On the other hand, there are some pretty unusual items, like Tuno and "soy brests," for those who want the sensation of tuna fish and chicken breasts without actually encountering fish and birds. The Native Foods vocabulary is indeed an ecclectic one, yet that doesn't keep the recipes from being straightforward and simple to execute.

But what I especially appreciate here is the lavish use of a very rare ingredient: joy. It's expressed in the goofy sense of humor, the energy, and the apparently limitless enthusiasm that accompanies Tanya in her mission to get everyone to eat well without eating a bite of anything to do with animals. It's hard to be consistently cheerful when faced with such a task, and the grimness that sometimes accompanies such missions can certainly get in the way of their success. At least it gets in the way of my interest. It's a great hook, but a hard one to come by. In fact, I've got some tempeh marinating in the fridge right now. But whether it's tempeh or a tomato, I do believe that if you seek out the freshest seasonal ingredients from one's farmers' market, then proceed to the kitchen armed with a sense of humor—

foreword

and joy—your food will be deeply good. Have no doubts. *The Native Foods Restaurant Cookbook* will definitely provide you with that cheerful nudge.

—Deborah Madison, author of
Vegetarian Cooking for Everyone
and *This Can't Be Tofu!*

acknowledgments

Thanks from the bottom of my heart to Gertrude and Peter Malch (a.k.a. Mom and Dad), whose careers and enjoyment in food and its service provided the finest training any school could have hoped to offer. I thank them for gracing me with the spirit of endurance that they had to learn during a childhood in Europe during World War II. I hope to use that spirit to try to offer the world a more compassionate palate.

Top-of-my-heart-felt thanks to Ray White, my founding Native business partner for bringing in that Native American spirit and who always believed in and loved me no matter what I came up with, and for hanging in when the pressure was on. Hold on, Ray! More to come!

Many blessings and thanks to the following:

Sam Bercholz, the magic door opener (I can't wait for the carpet ride!), and all the warm staff at Shambhala, including Eden Steinberg and especially my editor-magician Kendra Crossen Burroughs. Initially when I heard I had the best editor in the world, I didn't take it literally. Silly me, when a publisher says something, you have to take it literally!

Gloria Gallegos, my Chiquita, for tireless years and hours and who works "like she don't need the money," and all my incredible staff without which Native Foods could not exist, you know who you are. *¡Ustedes saben que los amo!* All the customers who have supported us through the years and to those of you who helped push out of the nest to make sure Westwood happened, and to all my cooking class students for taking time out to laugh, eat, and hopefully learn something!

All the chefs who unknowingly gave me lessons during my travels, including my grandmothers, the toothless fig woman in Yugoslavia, Roger Verge of Le Moulin de Mougins, my landlady in Kyoto, and the smiling cooking ladies in the beach huts in Thailand, to name a few.

My childhood gang of friends from four years old through high school, who have always been there for each other to support the joys and fears of our lives: Paula Lester Sacks, Megan Hanlon Akright, Pamela Levy Lubar, Ruth Arabella Sinfuego, Nancy Kokolj, Michael Avriette, Vida Rossi Dean.

Joanie Anderson, to whom, for passing on the art of making tempeh and seitan, I am forever grateful. If you love tempeh and seitan, then you have to love Joanie. . . . Hope you are feeling it, Joanie!

Barry Manilow for writing the songs and Garry Kief for getting them recorded so I have something to sing along with when I cook—they know you have to keep the cook happy.

Dr. Brian Bergstrom, a true renaissance man for recipe testing, and my study buddy and support while I wrote this. Whew, thank you again!

Laura Wilde, who took on recipe testing like she was grading her students' papers.

Loretta Swit for supporting a cruelty-free makeup line while helping me look better for the camera.

Mina Dovic, my macrobiotic savior, a.k.a. The Divine Miss Miso.

With loving thoughts and in memory of the impeccable listener Chistopher Weld, who was such a beacon to have had as a mentor from my early startup years. Many thanks to his beloved and my Goddess Guide, Mary Weld, who always helps me through the "moments."

Professor Thomas Azwell for eating vegan and sampling many of my tastings and also for teaching me what it's like to have a muse (by the way, I like it!).

Mary Lester for walking in the door at our seitan-making photo session and gifting us with a brand new All-Clad from the honorable Williams-Sonoma. How those photos now shine.

John Robbins, for your advice that was instrumental in the book's initial efforts and all that you have done along with the following group of souls in their roles of teaching and encouraging others to think inside and outside the lunchbox, that food is more than the few seconds it lasts in your mouth, and that those seconds are priceless: William Shurtleff and Akiko Aoyagi, Annemarie Colbin, Deborah Madison, Sunburst Farms Communities (from the '70s!, my first *natural* cookbook), Dana Jacobi, Mollie Katzen, Francis Moore Lappé, Mary Estella, Robin Robertson, Julie Child, Alice Waters, T. Colin Campbell, M.D., Dr. Michael Klapper, Dr. Dean Ornish, Dr. John McDougal, Ingrid Newkirk, Lorri and Gene Bauston, Jeff and Sabrina Nelson . . . and that's a partial list.

Patty Shenker, may the world remember your generosity and love and to everyone using their life skills to make the world a kindler and gentler place to live, may we one day hold all the coins in our pockets!

"The guys" that give Native Foods the style and pizazz that is a big part of our package, as good food has to have good looks around it: designers Bruce Goyers and Wayne Williamson (Insight West), Sam Cardella (Cardella Design), David Glomb (David Glomb Photography), Stephen Brogdon, the graphic designer mon (Brogdon Design), and Joe Vacek for the faultless fringe and technicolor touches.

Mathu Zephyr, a customer who wrote the Food Incantation that opens the book; we have copies of his poem posted in the restaurants. Mathu had been diagnosed with a possible terminal illness and in his regime of eating well became a regular at Native Foods. He has surprised and inspired many as he continues to live with renewed inspiration and zest for life.

A final thanks to all my dogs and cat for sitting around me and keeping my feet warm and the kitchen floors clean while I composed this book.

acknowledgments

introduction

In order to move in a positive direction for the future of our children, animals, the planet, health, and consciousness, the Western diet should be directed toward an organic vegetarian/vegan diet.

At Native Foods we have incorporated our experiences in food service, travel, and healthy cooking to offer you an ethnic fusion of bright colors, rich flavors, and delicious textures in a quick-service, stylish, fresh, and fun way.

In our menu concept we unite both the vegetarian and the traditional diner, and in doing so we specialize in introducing alternative tasty textures, which include tempeh and seitan. These foods have ancient origins, and making them—which we do from scratch—is a fine craft.

Our talent lies in bringing new artistry, creativity, and flair to vegetarian cuisine. We aim to transform the image of vegetarianism of the 1960s and 1970s into a delicious and enticing version for the twenty-first century.

Wishing you a prosperous lifestyle in harmony with the balance of nature and its energy through the wonders of food, and …

Thank you for having the courage to try something new!

Eat Peace,
The Natives

NATIVE FOODS AND ME

"If you can't stand the heat, get out of the kitchen." Family and friends in the restaurant business tried using that line to frighten me out of opening a restaurant, let alone an all-vegetarian one. They conjured up visions of too-difficult work and no money, problems with employees, quality-control worries, and "You'll have to add chicken and fish or you'll go out of business." The scare tactics didn't work. Having been born in the desert on a historically hot day of 125 degrees Fahrenheit, by the time I had my back to a huge oven making fresh pitas and vegetarian pizzas, I wasn't flinching.

Being raised in a hot climate not only brought new meaning to the term "home fries" but also instilled in my character a tenacity that, along with my family influences, prepared me to become a vegan restaurant entrepreneur.

My parents were European immigrants and worked in the restaurant business by default. Dad was rounded up from a soccer field by German soldiers as a teen in Yugoslavia and spent three years in a German labor camp. Mom was from a poor Czechoslovakian family and, as the eldest of six, cooked for all her siblings during the war years. She said that's why she only wanted one kid, so I'm an only child. If they'd had an opportunity to choose a career, my dad would have been an engineer and my mother an opera singer, which might have precluded producing a kitchen kid with an independent mind.

No matter their past, my parents are true "foodies." My father was a 5-star maître d', serving the last twenty years of his fifty-plus in the business at the exclusive Eldorado Country Club. My mother cooked like nobody's business day in and day out, and it was not your business until you were seated and the conversation was entirely about the meal and how it was prepared. Those who ate her meals, including friends and visiting dignitaries, said she made Julia Child look like a Taco Bell commercial. No offense to Julia—it was said purely as a tribute to Mom's gourmet skills (as a matter of fact, Julia's was one of Mom's favorite TV shows).

I have fond childhood memories of traveling to Europe with my parents. The first and last stop had to be Paris, so we could fill up on fine croissants and jams upon entry and take some home for breakfast in America. I'll never forget Dad with his list of delicacies to find in Paris, rushing to Fauchon, the greatest gourmet emporium on earth, to find a specific brand of Russian pickles, or waiting in line for bread at a boulangerie called Poilâne, which twenty years later would be overnighting to waiting customers in the States.

The French pastries were grand, but I couldn't wait to get to my grandmother's in Austria to add some weight (in knowledge and body mass) in that country's pastry skills! Picking blueberries in the Alps and then making dumplings was *wunderbar*! Then we'd head off to Yugoslavia for more family gatherings, where they would hide me when they delivered the freshly roasted suckling pig: "suckling" signifies a baby still nursing, and because of my love of animals, I could not have borne the sight of it. They didn't have to hide the stuffed pastry dishes of burek and gibanica, which were the cat's meow. (Actually the first word I learned in Yugoslavian was *muchka*, "cat." I even named my first cat Muchka.)

I thought this life centered around cooking and eating was great fun, but when I returned home and told friends about my summer adventures, they never quite got it, nor did their parents understand my "foodish" passion. Lunch to them was sandwiches of white bread and American cheese with mustard and mayonnaise, and try though I might, I never managed to like it. At that time America's dining repertoire was very limited. Fine dining was considered to be steak and lobster and baked potatoes. (This was before the era of Alice Waters, the star organic chef at Chez Panisse in Berkeley.) Thai restaurants were just beginning to gain popularity in major cities. Chinese food was the only established ethnic cuisine, and it was associated mainly with the crunchy fried noodle appetizer that you dipped in catsup and mustard.

Was I always a vegetarian? Not at all, but the way Europeans and most other traditional cultures eat includes lots of freshly prepared vegetables. On those trips to France, not only did I race to the Poilâne for bread but I had dreams of slathering it with a cheese of triple cream. It was that cat named Muchka, along with a rescued dog, that initiated the love for animals that evolved in the formative years of my childhood. On another summer trip to France, while petting the dairy cows on a family farm, I learned what happens when a male baby is born. That calf gets renamed, and that name is veal! I returned to junior high school that fall, and for one class we had to do a report on crime. I chose the first topic on the list, "cruelty to animals." This led to reading about the whaling industry and veal production in this country. Talk about eye-opening. For an outlet of expression and to help the animals, I founded and became president of the Friends of Animals club. I was starting to think seriously about what I was eating, and thereby hangs a tale.

I went vegetarian at eighteen. I was told to by everyone who was really concerned about me to read everything on the topic before making such a decision. They feared I wouldn't get my protein and calcium, and believed that you just plain needed meat juice. Obviously they didn't read the material they suggested I must; if they had, they would have jumped ship with me and would have never had a worry. Their scare tactics and teasing angered me a bit at first, but I have since softened and am thankful for their advice, which only served to strengthen my argument.

I loved plants, I loved animals, and I got turned on to yoga by PBS (in the days when you'd say "yoga" and people would say "Oh, stretching"). At UC Santa Cruz I chose a major in biology and met my housemate Joanie Anderson. Joanie loved to cook French cuisine but went macrobiotic for health reasons and ate mostly vegetarian. It is here that the lights shone down from heaven and the dance began as Joanie introduced me to the crafts of making tempeh and seitan and the history of macrobiotics. Reading about macrobiotics while studying chemistry was really chemistry!

Once I had gained the knowledge of tempeh and seitan, the vision started solidifying: by adding some great textures and flavors, one could create a menu for a vegetarian restaurant that even the most avid carnivore would enjoy. Having been warned about the restaurant business, I continued to contemplate other career choices, like pre-med, exercise physiology, marine biology, and botany. While mulling over these life decisions, I found myself cooking quite often, as a kind of stress relief, and it became a great way to make friends away from home. I still couldn't shake off the vegetarian restaurant idea.

There were adventures and business ventures in between this thoughtful time and the final realization of my vision, including a year in Japan, Korea, Thailand, Malaysia, and Indonesia, and meeting my partner, Ray White (a.k.a. Chief Whitefeather). Ray got hooked on a tempeh sandwich after being a confirmed meat-and-potatoes restaurateur in L.A. As Ray now says, "Once you learn the right way of eating, and love it, why turn back?" Once craving only steaks, now he only craves Native! Yeah, Ray!

In 1994 we opened the first Native Foods Restaurant in Palm Springs in a breezeway of a shopping center. I knew it would work, because when I was opening the door for the first time, I looked up and saw a dove's nest complete with cooing family—a good omen, I was sure! I had finally created a job for myself working in all the compassionate areas I enjoy: health, animals, saving the environment, and food service.

A year later we opened a second location in Palm Desert, not too far away but a good distance, to try the "operating more than one store" idea. By the time the phone rang with news of the availability of a Los Angeles location (Westwood Village), we were ready! Now as this book is being written, our Mongolian yurt–designed restaurant is being built in Costa Mesa, California (close to Disneyland—come visit!).

Native Foods restaurants exist to showcase a progressive, high-quality vegetarian cuisine that is nutritious, organic, compassionate, and delicious. The thought behind the "Native Foods" name is "indigenous to the earth and low on the food chain." Our restaurant does have Native American spirit, owing to Ray's heritage (he's a Nipmuc from the Alquonquin Nation), but the menu is eclectic and multicultural. We seek to offer a little bit of everything to everyone. I have long had the desire to encourage Americans to discover and enjoy tempeh and seitan, which, along with the textured soy proteins, are protein-rich alternatives for carnivores or just a fun new food experience for the adventurous. Native Foods is a place where people of all food orientations can get together and have an enjoyable, healthy, and friendly meal.

Since the first Native Foods restaurant began, there have been numerous requests from customers and cooking-class students for a cookbook, so here it is! I hope that you will find this book easy to use, learn something new, invite friends for dinner parties, and help educate the world that eating vegetarian can be exciting, exotic, erotic, tasty, and definitely not boring rabbit food. Most of all, have fun and laugh and sing while you are trying the recipes, because that's something you do taste but can't be written in recipes.

THE VEGETARIAN LIFESTYLE

Why people choose a vegan or vegetarian lifestyle varies. Most reasons fall into the following categories.

Health. Vegetarians are always asked how they get their protein or how they get their nutrition. I am amazed that this question isn't commonly posed to the millions of people who eat regularly at fast-food establishments. What would they be able to answer? How does eating an El Chicken Burrito or Busto Beefy Burger fulfill their nutritional requirements?

Yes, the word is out, the evidence is strong: eating a balanced vegetarian diet is healthiest! If you've already got one of the top five health problems (heart disease, cancer, type 2 diabetes, high blood pressure, obesity), a vegetarian diet can help heal.

Just look what success Dr. Dean Ornish has had with his reversal of heart disease programs that include, among other things, a low-fat vegetarian diet. It worked for over 70 percent of his patients. The National Cancer Institute has said that one third of all cancers are diet-related. Colon cancer is growing rapidly in this country, especially in women. The American Dietetic Association has said that people eating balanced vegetarian diets have lower rates of type 2 diabetes.

Personally I've watched many middle-aged people come to the restaurant a little bummed because they got the high blood pressure and/or high cholesterol verdict and were told to begin eating better. Usually, within thirty days of their

A DIVINE SPARK

"Even in the worm that crawls in the earth there glows a divine spark. When you slaughter a creature, you slaughter God."
—Isaac Bashevis Singer, vegetarian and Nobel Prize–winning writer

switch to vegetarianism we are "high-fiving" each other after the doctor told them their numbers were back within the healthy and hopeful range.

Obesity now affects 27 percent of Americans, and 61 percent are overweight. Kids are feeling it too more than ever and increasingly are being diagnosed with type 2 diabetes, usually found in middle-aged people. Given that kids drink more soda pop than water, it's no small wonder.

Another health consideration: It is now conceded that antibiotics fed to animals in farm production are the main cause of antibiotic resistance in people, and bacteria in these environments are evolving to surive. *E. coli* is a factor to be reckoned with daily by meat eaters.

Ethics. Many vegetarians are motivated by an ethical objection to the cruelty of commercial methods of raising animals for food (factory farming), or by a strong spiritual conviction that to exploit, hurt, or kill any living creature is wrong. Love and compassion for animals was my own entry into the vegetarian lifestyle. One drive on a freeway behind a chicken truck with cages piled on top of each other containing miserable chickens on the way to slaughter, and knowing that they had lived out their short lives in a space no larger than an 8 x 11–inch sheet of notebook paper, is enough to motivate many to become vegetarians. Or seeing an undercover video of workers saying that cows often get hung on a hook and skinned and have their feet removed while they are still conscious. Or hearing a dairy farmer say that the hardest thing is separating the baby calves from their mothers, as both mother and baby cry to get back together. The separation is imposed so that the mother can go on to produce milk for human consumption and not for her baby.

When there are fun and good, healthy ways to eat without causing such pain and suffering, why not eat compassionately?

Environment. The devastation of the environment that results from a meat-centered diet is alarming. Just consider that to get one pound of beef from a feedlot requires somewhere around 2,500 gallons of water (that's about six months' worth of showering). Factory farms produce massive amounts of manure waste that damages local water supplies, as do pesticides and nitrates from chemical fertilizers used in agriculture. Combine that with the five million acres of rainforest that are destroyed in Central and South America each year to create pastures for cattle, and the fact that while fish sizes and populations are declining worldwide, one third of fish caught in the seas are ground up and used as cattle feed. The equation isn't balancing.

Economics. Waste is never a good thing to end up with in any business economy. The trick is to end up with as little waste or nonusable product as possible. Now, if you produce a waste that is counterproductive to the lifestyle you wish to lead—such as creating toxic environments as opposed to living in beauty and serenity—you have to enter that into the bottom line somehow. To me, that would be a negative. If I kill a river with pesticides that I used to grow crops to feed people, those actions cancel each other out. If it takes 1.2 gallons of oil to make the chemical fertilizer for a bushel of corn, then a corn-fed cow, slaughtered at 1,200 pounds, has used 284 gallons oil to produce the amount of corn eaten. Compare that to the relatively small edible portion of the cow and the nutritional value one could get from that versus the corn itself, and see why these negative equations are starting to be recognized in the economic world. The economic sensibility seems to be a minor reason people are turning toward or embracing a complete or partial vegetarian lifestyle for themselves, but it is a significant reason why major corporations are lending an ear. When demand for a product or service increases, businesses increase to accommodate that demand.

So who chooses to go veg for the above reasons? My impression from years of working in the restaurant business is that most of the older adults and those of the baby-boomer generation who are vegetarians follow this lifestyle for the health benefits. For the younger generations of X and Y (and, I predict, for their children), it is for the ethical and environmental reasons. So if you think the younger generation has gone down the drain, relax. They are not crazy, just compassionate, and what they do with their lives will greatly improve the planet and everyone's quality of life.

....

FOR MORE INFORMATION: For specifics about the health, ethical, and other issues related to vegetarianism, I recommend two books by John Robbins, *Diet for a New America: How Your Food Choices Affect Your Health, Happiness, and the Future of Life on Earth* and *The Food Revolution: How Your Diet Can Help Save Your Life and Our World.* Also check out the web site www.vegsource.com.

....

Definitions

Most people I meet in Native Foods are trying to eat better and haven't necessarily put a "name tag" on it yet. Everyone is on a journey. These labels just help give direction to where they might like to go. The comedian Kevin Nealon, when asked about his eating style, once described himself as a "cheatin' vegan"—a great response, I thought, acknowledging that embracing a lifestyle that is not mainstream (at least not yet; I'm working on it!) is difficult at times to maintain.

Omnivore   Someone who eats both vegetables and animals.

Carnivore   Someone who eats mostly flesh from animals.

Vegetarian   A person who doesn't eat anything with a face or a mother! A vegetarian may consume animal by-products such as dairy and eggs but doesn't eat red meat, poultry, or fish. The common question years ago was whether you were ovo, lacto, or lacto-ovo. *Ovo* refers to eating eggs, *lacto* refers to dairy, and *lacto-ovo* refers to eating both. No one really asks that anymore. The trend is moving from vegetarianism into veganism.

Vegan   (usually pronounced *VEE-gun*) A vegetarian who consumes no animal products or by-products at all (including foods such as honey) and often will not wear or use cosmetics or apparel derived from animals. Vegans are thus careful not to wear wool, silk, or leather—and no, they aren't starving or running around naked with dirty feet!

Dictator   A strong-willed person who rules with absolute power. Try not to become one even if you think eating one way is better than another!

....

ARE HUMANS NATURALLY CARNIVOROUS? Try this test. When driving down the highway and you spot some road kill, check your appetite. Does your mouth start watering? Do you immediately pull in to the first fast-food drive-thru?

Compare that to when you are driving by a field of peach or cherry orchards or berry fields with a sign saying "You pick," or when you see a fresh-fruit stand by the side of the road. Do you get the urge to pull over and start picking or eating the fruit?

A lion would probably pick the road kill. My kids would probably pick the fruit.

....

PASSIONATE ABOUT ORGANICS

Native Foods strives to serve all organic products. Some produce items can be cost-prohibitive for our already set menu prices, but we regularly obtain organic grains, beans, and flours. I prefer you use all organic ingredients when trying the recipes in this cookbook.

Organic agricultural products are grown without toxic pesticides and fertilizers and are farmed by methods that maintain and replenish the nutrition of the soil.

Organic foods are organic agricultural products minimally processed without artificial ingredients, preservatives, or irradiation.

"Certified Organic" began as a third-party certification from either a state or private organization. These included strict standards, inspections, and testing of farm lands and processing facilities.

Throughout the years, state and national groups have been meeting to set a standard certification that wouldn't vary from state to state and that would enforce such standards. In 1990 the Organic Food Production Act (OFPA) was set up by the federal government. They then set up a National Organic Standards Board to develop guidelines and procedures to regulate all organic crops.

In December 2000 the U.S. Department of Agriculture decided to implement the OFPA of 1990, and it went into full effect as of October 2002. Now any foods labeled "organic" must meet these standards.

Does that mean all foods labeled organic have no pesticide residues? Not necessarily, since North America has for the past fifty years overused chemicals, which are found in rain and groundwater (yes, we finally did it), but buying organic now will help stop new contamination of our water. In some cities in high agricultural areas, the herbicide and pesticide levels found in tap water are health-threatening.

Organic sometimes costs more, but you, your body, your health, and your family are worth it! Set your standards high when it comes to what you allow in your body. A 99-cent burrito may look like a good deal on the outside, but it's a bad deal for your inside.

Concerned citizens can change the tide with our buying power by purchasing organic. As my friend Howard Lyman, a former farmer, once said, "Let the organic farmer get rich—then everyone will grow organic."

Praise organic farmers! If you see them at a farmers' market, thank them, buy an extra peach, tip them, and oh, why not, send one of their kids to college! Soon they may return the favor, as the sales of organic food was $5.4 billion in 1998 and $7.8 billion by 2000. This market grew 20 to 24 percent annually in the 1990s.

Organic is not a fad, it's a revolution.

ORGANIC TASTES BETTER. How can I express the distinctive feeling of organic? There is nothing like opening a box of organic produce compared with conventional nonorganic—it has a vibe all its own. You can also tell the difference when you cut the vegetable and feel it, and of course the taste is better too. It's a kind of exciting sense of vitality and pure flavor. Try visiting the organic section at a farmer's market sometime and find out for yourself!

part one

The Basics

the setup

KNOW YOUR INGREDIENTS: A GLOSSARY OF FOODS

This glossary includes foods that might be new to some readers, to make the information about them available at a quick glance. If you are looking for a specific food that's not here, please see the index.

adzuki beans   Small Japanese red beans. Also spelled *azuki*. See page 52.

agar   Also known as agar-agar, because it's good-good. It's a sea vegetable origin and is rich in iodine, calcium, and other minerals. When cooked with liquid, it makes a gel, hence it is vegetarian gelatin. Agar generally comes in flakes or in compressed bars in the Asian markets, and is also found in powdered form—all clear in color. Powdered agar is great because it dissolves fast, but many markets don't carry it, though it is commonly used by professional bakers and pastry chefs. Flakes are used in this book, as they are the most readily available. About 2 teaspoons of agar flakes will firmly gel 1 cup of liquid.

CRUELTY-FREE GELATIN. Agar is a vegetarian alternative to gelatin, which comes from the hooves, bones, and skin of animals—basically slaughterhouse waste. One restaurant customer who is an interior designer told me about a young client who was redecorating his New York apartment with the finest of fine. Curious about his successful lifestyle, she asked what he did for a living, and he told her he sold animal hides from Asia to the Jell-O company. Fact or fiction? In either case, the real question to ask: Did your dessert once wiggle?

....

amaranth   A high-protein grain. See page 57.

apple cider vinegar   Vinegar made from apple cider has a sweet but pleasant acidic bite.

arame   A delightful sea vegetable with a mellow flavor. It reconstitutes quickly. You can just soak and toss in salads or soups.

arrowroot   A starchy powder made from a tuberous root, used for thickening sauces, gravies, and desserts. One tablespoon will thicken a cup of liquid.

avocado   A rich and creamy green fruit native to the tropics and sub-tropics. The majority are now grown in California. There are several varieties, which have slightly different flesh textures ranging from a very buttery (higher oil content) to a slightly firmer and more watery texture. The Haas avocado is one of the creamier varieties and is recognized by its dark-colored, rough skin; it is the most popular among chefs and aficionados. Other varieties include the Fuerte (with a thin, smooth, lighter green skin), Reed, Bacon, and Pinkerton.

azuki beans   See adzuki beans.

balsamic vinegar   (*bal-SAH-mik*) A distinctly flavored, sweet vinegar made from certain grapes from the Modena area of Italy and aged in various woods. Recipes vary from producer to producer.

bancha tea   A Japanese green tea with very low caffeine content. Bancha makes a good, light everyday tea. A similar beverage, made from just the twigs of the tea plant, is known as kukicha. Roasted bancha is called hojicha.

barley malt syrup   A natural alternative to sugar and honey, this light liquid sweetener is made from germinated barley.

barley tea, roasted	A steeped drink made from roasted barley that has been simmered in water.
brests	*See* soy brests.
bulgur	Cracked wheat, sometimes known as wheat pilaf.
caper	A berry with a tangy, pungent flavor. The caper bush is native to the Mediterranean and some parts of Asia. Capers range in size from small to something called a caperberry, which is the size of an olive. They usually come packed in brine but can also be found packed in salt.
cardamom	A delightfully aromatic East Indian spice. The little black seeds inside the dried pod are ground into a powder. The whole pod is often used in cooking and then removed before serving.
chestnut	A large brown nut grown on trees in Asia, Europe, and the United States. Chestnuts are commonly roasted, boiled, braised, or baked to remove the outer skin, and the sweet flesh is prepared in numerous ways as a dessert or in savory dishes. They can be bought fresh when in season and also found canned or bottled, plain or sweetened. Chestnuts are also dried and ground into a flour.
chickpeas	*See* garbanzo beans, page 52.
chili	There are many varieties of chili pepper, all of the *Capsicum* genus, that extend throughout all the continents of the world. The chilies used in this book include the following. The *Anaheim*, named after the city in California (Disneyland's hometown), is long and green and has a mild flavor. The red variety of the Anaheim is called *Chile Colorado*. The *jalapeño*, common in Mexican cuisine, is a small (thumb-sized), mostly dark green pepper that is usually quite hot. *Chipotle* is a smoked jalapeño chile that can be found dried or canned with vinegar and salt.

chili powder	Any dried and ground chili, but most commonly as a powdered blend that contains dried chilies as well as garlic, oregano, cumin, coriander, and sometimes cloves.
cilantro	Cilantro is the Spanish name for the herb that some call coriander leaf or Chinese parsley. It is best used fresh and not dried. Cilantro's distinct flavor appears often in Mexican and Asian cuisine. I've noticed that people either love it or hate it—and that some people who at first didn't like it go absolutely mad for it down the road.
coconut, dried	Dried coconut is obtained from the white flesh of a mature coconut. It is usually found shredded or flaked and comes either sweetened or unsweetened. The recipes in this book call for the unsweetened product.
coconut milk	This is made by cooking the shredded flesh of the coconut in coconut water and then straining it. It is most easily used canned. Try to get the kind without added preservatives and definitely with no sugar added, which would make it way too sweet for most culinary purposes.
coriander	The dried seed from cilantro flowers. It is available whole or ground, and its flavor is a totally different flavor from that of fresh cilantro leaves.
corn flour	Finely ground cornmeal. If you have only cornmeal and want corn flour, you can grind cornmeal in the blender.
cornstarch	A powdery flour made from the endosperm (center) of the corn kernel. It is used as a thickening agent in liquid ingredients. Sauces thickened with cornstarch will be clear with a fine sheen. To use cornstarch, you must first dissolve it in cold water and then stir it into the hot liquid to be thickened.
couscous	Steamed, dried, and cracked grains made from the kind of wheat used for pasta. Couscous is finer in texture and lighter in color than bulgur wheat. Although white couscous

is the most common variety, the grain also comes in a whole wheat version.

cucumber
This member of the gourd family comes in different varieties. *Conventional* cucumbers are usually waxed, so it's advisable to peel them before use. The seeds can be large and slightly bitter, so they are usually removed. The crunchy *Japanese* cucumber is smaller in diameter than a conventional cucumber, and it has smaller seeds, so there is no need to remove the seeds before eating. *Hothouse* cucumbers, also known as *English* cucumbers, are very long and have very small seeds that don't need to be removed before enjoying.

cumin
A dried seed spice available either whole or ground. In East Indian markets, you may see black cumin, which is quite different from the familiar cumin or comino that many use for Mexican cooking. The cumin used in our recipes resembles a caraway seed but has a stronger, more aromatic flavor.

curry powder
A blend of East Indian spices that usually includes turmeric powder, which gives curry powder its yellow color. I've found the commercially available curry blends not to be very spicy. In India, every household grinds their own spice mixtures fresh, and prepared curry powder is rarely used. I usually start with a commercial blend and add more of my favorite Indian spices to it.

daikon
A Japanese white radish that is usually about 12 inches long and looks like a big white carrot. In this book it appears in soups, but it can also be used for salads and side dishes. In macrobiotics, it is said to help dissolve fat and mucus deposits in the body.

edamame
(*ed-ah-MAH-meh*) Green soybeans right out of the pod, eaten raw, roasted and seasoned, or boiled for stews or healing teas. See page 135.

Egg Substitute	An egg substitute is sometimes used in vegan baking for its binding quality. (Eggs contain the protein albumin, which helps create a light texture while binding ingredients in baked goods.) The recipe for Egg Substitute used in this book (see below) I learned from Abbot George Burke. There is also a product on the market called Egg Replacer that can be used.

....

EGG SUBSTITUTE FOR BAKING. Mix together 2 Tbsp vital gluten flour (see below under "gluten flour"), ½ tsp baking powder, and 2 Tbsp water. Don't let it sit too long before you use it. This is the equivalent of one egg.

....

filo	An Eastern European and Middle Eastern pastry dough made by creating paper-thin sheets of flour and water.
garbanzo beans	Legumes also known as chickpeas, the main ingredient in hummus. See page 52.
ginger	A root that imparts a pungent, slightly sweet, peppery flavor. Ginger is common in Jamaican, Indian, and East Asian cuisine, and is also made into a tea as a remedy for such ailments as nausea, stomachache, and headache, or used as a poultice for external wounds. It is used in its fresh root form and may also be pickled with rice vinegar and sugar and used as a sweet condiment. Dried ginger is commonly used in baking and has a completely different flavor than fresh ginger. You can't substitute one for the other in recipes—it is that different. Crystallized (or candied) ginger is made by boiling fresh ginger in a sugar syrup and then coating it with sugar.
gluten flour	(also called vital gluten flour, pure gluten flour, or vital wheat gluten) Wheat flour that has the starch removed and is purely protein. It is not the same as "high-gluten flour,"

which is just a flour with higher protein content. Gluten flour holds moisture and produces greater pliability in breads. It is also used in the seitan recipe in this book.

green onions   An onion variety also known as spring onions or scallions. The above-ground green portion is eaten as well as the bulb, in contrast to other types of onions.

hemp seeds   Hemp seeds come from the *Cannabis* species but have only trace quantities of THC (the chemical that makes marijuana intoxicating). Industrial hemp has been harvested for over twelve thousand years for food and fiber. It is high in vitamin E and iron and linoleic acid, an omega-3 fatty acid. Hemp seeds can be purchased hulled and toasted slightly for a distinctive nutty flavor.

herbs de Provence   A mixture of dried herbs from the regions of southern France. Usually it contains marjoram, savory, fennel, basil, thyme, and lavender.

hijiki   A sea vegetable with a wiry appearance and a jet-black color when dried. Since hijiki is a little strong in flavor, it needs to be rinsed and cooked with soy sauce and rice vinegar. Then it makes a really tasty and nutritious side dish.

jicama   (*HEE-ca-muh*) The tuberous root of a Mexican plant. It is very crunchy, sweet, and watery in taste and whitish in color.

kasha   Cooked buckwheat groats.

kombu   A wide, thick, green sea vegetable. *Kombu* is the Japanese name for this species of kelp. By adding it to beans and grains when cooking, we add a boost of minerals to them.

kuzu   The powder of a starchy root used as a thickening agent similar to arrowroot. It dilutes quickly in cold water and has a great smooth finishing texture. If you don't have kuzu, you may substitute equal amounts of cornstarch or arrowroot.

KUZU GALORE. The kuzu plant was imported decades ago from Japan to the southeastern United States, where it became known as kudzu. Initially the plant was promoted for ornamental gardening, animal feed, and erosion control. However, the vine grew too well in the South and spread uncontrollably over everything it encountered, so that today many Southerners tell stories of their desperate attempts to either kill kudzu (which can damage trees) or find creative new uses for it. I wish they'd powder the root and promote it for culinary use—the kuzu sold in American natural food stores as a thickening agent is a little expensive, as most of it comes from Japan. In addition to its use in cooking, kuzu is held to possess medicinal benefits in macrobiotics.

lavosh (*LAH-vohsh*) A flatbread available in Middle Eastern or Armenian markets and natural food stores. It may be thin and crisp or soft and pliable.

leavening Substances such as baking powder, baking soda, and yeast that leaven, or lighten the texture and increase the volume of, baked goods.

lemon grass A lemony-scented and -flavored grass used in Asian (especially Thai) dishes and beverages.

lotus root The root of a beautiful water lily often depicted in Eastern spiritual art. The root has the texture of a potato and has hollow sections through its length so when sliced in a cross-section it looks like a cut-out flower pattern, unusual and pretty.

maple syrup This syrup produced from the sap of the sugar maple tree is a friendlier sugar to the body than cane sugar, as it has traces of minerals and B vitamins. It contains only about 65 percent sucrose as opposed to 99.5 percent in processed white sugar. (Sucrose leads to overproduction of insulin, thus placing a heavy demand on the pancreas, so the less sucrose in the diet, the better.) Several grades of maple syrup are available. Most commonly at the markets I find grade A or grade B. Grade A is lighter in color and has a more delicate flavor, while grade B has a stronger, deeper flavor. I like to use grade B in cooking and baking because of its flavor.

margarine A butter alternative made from vegetable oils. Not all brands are vegan; sometimes dairy additives such as whey are used. Many brands contain hydrogenated oils, which may contain trans fatty acids (known to raise levels of "bad" cholesterol and decrease "good" cholesterol levels). Earth Balance is a great brand that is free of trans fatty acids and has a good flavor.

mayonnaise, vegan Usually mayonnaise is made from an emulsion of vegetable oil, egg yolks, and lemon juice or vinegar. There are two brands currently available that are vegan and use soy protein to help emulsify instead of egg yolks. One is Nayonnaise and the other is Vegannaise. The latter has a richer, creamer texture and is more comparable to a thick mayonnaise.

millet A lovely little round yellow grain, very high in iron. See pages 58 and 62.

miso A fermented paste made of soybeans and/or grains that is a tasty condiment used in Japanese and macrobiotic-style dishes. It contains essential amino acids, minerals, and B vitamins, and is low in fat.

....

MANY MISOS. Miso comes in many varieties and colors. It is almost always based on soybeans, which may be mixed with rice or other grains before a culture (called *koji*) and a little sea salt are added, whereupon the mixture is aged at a cool temperature to create a smooth or grainy product. The finer misos are aged at least two to three years. I recommend starting with the mildest variety, a light white miso (which has a sweet, creamy taste) and trying the darker, more aged misos, with their saltier, stronger flavors, as you become more of a miso connoisseur.

....

mung beans A small green bean that is often used in East Indian cuisine. See page 53.

olive oil Oil from olives! Extra-virgin olive oil should be used as a condiment or a final touch to flavor dishes; it has too heavy and strong a flavor for most cooking. Most olive oils that are labeled "virgin" are fine for cooking. "Pure" olive oil is more processed but still without solvents. The "light" or "lite" labeling of olive oil is just a marketing ploy to sell low-grade olive oil, refined probably with the use of solvents. The color is light and has nothing to do with the fat content, which is the same as any other oil.

quinoa (*KEEN-wah*) A high-protein grain. See pages 59 and 62.

rice flour Flour made by grinding raw rice into a powder.

rice vinegar Vinegar made from rice has a light and delicate flavor and a low acid content. Brown rice vinegar is more nutritious but has a deeper flavor than vinegar made from white rice.

safflower oil Oil made from the seeds of the safflower plant. The recipes in this book that use safflower oil call for the refined variety, which is pale in color. The darker, unrefined oil would impart an overly strong flavor. Look for a brand such as Spectrum, whose refined oils are processed without chemicals, unlike the commercial brands.

sea salt Salt mined from the sea, if not too refined, will have more minerals in it and a softer and sweeter finish in the taste, compared with processed 99.9 percent NaCl (sodium chloride), or regular table salt. Believe me, you can taste the difference.

sea vegetables   Americans are just starting to eat some of the many types, thanks to the influence of Japanese cuisine and restaurants. Among the sea vegetables used in this book are wakame, arame, agar, and kombu (kelp).

seitan   (*SAY-tan*) The meaty-textured protein of wheat, made by kneading a wheat flour dough. See the "Seitan" chapter, page 66.

sesame   This seed has been grown widely throughout Asia and India since ancient times. There are different varieties of different colors ranging from browns to black and to red; they vary only slightly in flavor but all have the pronounced sesame taste. The most common is a light tan color, which when hulled appears white. The seeds have a high oil content and will turn rancid quickly, so store in tight containers in a cool place and use often.

sesame oil, toasted   A dark brown sesame oil that imparts a special nutty flavor. It is sold in small bottles, as it is used mainly for seasoning.

shortening, vegetable   A solid fat produced from vegetable oils, usually made by hydrogenating the oils and thereby creating the not-so-healthy trans fatty acids. Spectrum and Earth Balance are brands of organic shortening that do not contain trans fatty acids.

soba   A traditional Japanese buckwheat noodle.

soy brests   These soy "chicken" breasts, a high-protein textured soy product, are available through The Mail Order Catalog for Healthy Eating in Summertown, Tennessee. Tel.: (800) 695-2241. Web site: www.healthy-eating.com (where the product is called "Chiken Brests").

soy cream cheese   A nondairy cream cheese. The most flavorful brand is Tofutti, which is becoming increasingly available at major retail markets. It does contain some hydrogenated fats, so if that concerns you, don't use it often or save it for special occasions.

soy milk   A high-protein "milk" made from cooked soybeans and water.

soy sauce   The liquid created when soybeans, wheat, water, and sea salt are aged for a period of time. There are quick and cheaper methods to make soy sauce, but they don't taste as good and aren't as good for you. Avoid soy sauce with added alcohol, and try to find naturally brewed brands. *See also* tamari.

soy sour cream   A nondairy sour cream. Tofutti brand is the one I recommend. It is usually carried by the markets that carry the Tofutti cream cheese.

spelt berries   The whole kernels of an ancient species of wheat. Some people with wheat allergies can enjoy spelt instead of wheat. See the table on page 62 for cooking directions.

sugar   Organic cane sugar is used in the recipes in this book. It is not bleached, so it is not superwhite in color.

Some brands of cane sugar use a charcoal filtration processing to obtain a product that will have almost no residue when dissolved in water; why that's so important I'm not sure, but the charcoal used is often from animal bone. This is not acceptable for many vegans, who avoid white sugar for this reason. When sugar is nonorganic, not only may the fields impart pesticide residue, which is harmful to the workers and consumers, but the fields are often burned and the chemicals can then be released into the air, creating another hazard.

Sucanat and Rapadura are two brands of sugar that are basically just the cane juice dried without separating the molasses from the dried final product. Molasses sugar contains a higher molasses content and is darker. I recommend trying maple sugar and date sugar in baking and cooking, for variety.

Powdered sugar is finely ground cane sugar with corn-starch added. An organic powdered sugar has recently been marketed by Hain.

sun-dried tomatoes   Vine-ripened tomatoes dried naturally in the sun. They are sold either dried in a package or packed in oil. I prefer to reconstitute the dried tomatoes by placing them in a small bowl and adding hot water to cover for about 15–20 minutes, until soft.

sunflower oil   Oil produced from the seeds of those big, beautiful flowers. The kind recommended for the recipes is refined. Look for a brand such as Spectrum, whose refined oils are processed without chemicals, unlike the commercial brands.

tabouli   A Middle Eastern dish served as a cold salad, traditionally made with bulghur wheat, chopped tomatoes, onions, mint, parsley, olive oil, and lemon juice.

tahini   A paste made of ground sesame seeds; also known as sesame butter.

tamari   Traditionally, tamari was the thick brown liquid that was poured off when miso finished fermenting. A way was then invented to make it in quantity without making miso first, and that became soy sauce. It was typically made with soy-beans and wheat. In America a soy sauce made without wheat (using only soybeans, water, and salt) became known as tamari. A natural aging process should be used in its manufacture, so avoid tamari with added alcohol or preservatives, as this indicates that a "quick" brew has taken place and not the quality aging process of at least one year.

teff   A tough, tiny grain of Ethiopian origin, high in protein and calcium. It is apparently the smallest grain in the world.

tempeh   A cultured food made of soybeans, usually with a grain or two added. See the "Tempeh" chapter, page 63.

tofu	The "cheese" made from soy milk. Tofu is available in soft, medium, and firm, and sometimes extra-firm, and also in two basic styles, silken and Chinese. See "How Do You Do Tofu?" on page 78.
tomatillo	This vegetable (it's a fruit, technically) looks like a small green tomato in a paper skin. It imparts a tangy flavor, which some have called plumlike, to Mexican and Southwestern dishes.
Tuno	The brand name of a soy-based tuna substitute produced by Worthington Foods (a Kellogg company).
turmeric	This root is from the same family as ginger, which it resembles when fresh. We usually see it dried in its powder form. Intensely yellow, it is the spice that gives curry its distinctive color. Turmeric has a slightly bitter flavor, so it must be used sparingly when added for natural coloring.
udon	A type of Japanese noodle. In Japan it is commercially seen as a fat, round wheat noodle, but in American natural food stores it is a brown rice noodle, and that is what we use in this book.
umeboshi	A tart Japanese plum that is usually dried, then pickled in salt brine. In Asia it is used medicinally and as a tangy food condiment. Its pink color is due to the red shiso (herb) leaves used in the pickling process. Umeboshi can be purchased as whole plums, as a paste, or in vinegar form.

• •

UMEBOSHI PLUMS. This favorite seasoning of macrobiotic cuisine is valued for its "yang" qualities. Umeboshi is high in alkaline minerals, such as iron and magnesium, and is also rich in citric acid, which is what you need to help the body absorb these minerals. A natural synergistic food combo! Japanese traditional medicine says that umeboshi strengthens the blood (by breaking down excess acid) and is beneficial to liver and kidney function.

....

vital gluten flour — See gluten flour.

wakame — A sea vegetable commonly used in miso soup. It has a thin leafy consistency. Traditional Asian medicine use it to purify the blood and regards it as beneficial to women's reproductive health.

wheat berries — The whole kernels of wheat, before they are ground into flour. See page 62.

yeast, nutritional — A palatable yeast, not as bitter as brewer's yeast and not the same as baker's yeast for making bread. Nutritional yeast usually comes in flake form, though it's also available as a powder. It's a source of vitamin B_{12} and has a cheeselike flavor. Some people like to toss a little on salads and on popcorn for a cheesy effect. It's also used in our nondairy cheese recipe (Native Ch'i's, page 97).

zest — The flavorful rind of a citrus fruit. See page 48.

THE WELL-EQUIPPED KITCHEN: A GLOSSARY OF UTENSILS

These are items that will set up a basic beginning kitchen enabling you to make the recipes in this book. You can add more equipment later when you expand your repertoire of cooking.

Pots 'n' Pans

When was the last time you decided what kind of pot to buy? Today there are many choices to choose from, such as copper, aluminum, stainless steel, and cast iron. "Touch, feel, and use" is the best advice for finding the pot that suits you best.

I recommend a heavy-gauge stainless steel such as 18/10. Look for a thick bottom that has aluminum or copper in between the layers of stainless, as this helps retain heat better than a solely stainless bottom. Solid metal handles that are bolted on are better than the plastic screw-in kind. The most reputable and well-built (and expensive) brand that you can find in most stores is the All-Clad. My mother's 2-quart that she's had for twenty-five years has been used a lot and still looks great, so there is that advantage of buying high-quality ware. Calphalon is a nice-quality brand too, but if you need more of a bargain, shop around; there might be a set on sale that can get you started, and you can always upgrade as you begin to cook more often.

I think cast iron is a good choice too, and very reasonable. The more you use it, the better it cooks, but it doesn't come in many styles and sizes, and it's heavy, so I suggest one skillet or griddle for starters.

Avoid Teflon-coated pans. You can't get a decent searing edge on the food with them, you can't use metal utensils in them because it scratches off the surface (which scratches off anyway after a while), and I don't think that the scratched-off particles are good to ingest. Moreover, the American Veterinary Medical Association web site warns that Teflon (and Silverstone) fumes are highly toxic to small animals and especially hazardous to pet birds that are exposed to them.

Here are the recommended basics:

- 10-inch skillet
- 3-quart saucepan
- 5-quart saucepan
- 10-inch cast-iron griddle (for making French toast and heating corn tortillas)

Bakeware

The items listed here should serve all all your oven needs. Look for heavy aluminum, and avoid the coated variety.

- 9-inch pie pan
- 1 or 2 aluminum cookie sheets
- 13 x 9 x 2–inch baking pan
- 9 x 5 x 3–inch loaf pan
- 8 x 8–inch square cake pan
- 9-inch round cake pan
- wire cooling racks
- good-quality oven mitts

Bowls

- nest of four or five mixing bowls. Stainless steel is light and easy to clean.

Measurement

Until you're an experienced enough cook to add ingredients by intuition, use these!

- measuring spoon set
- dry measure set (stainless steel cups with handles that come in ¼, ⅓, ½, and 1 cup measures)
- 2-cup liquid measuring cup

Knives

You'll probably want to get a high-carbon steel knife, as it does not discolor and is easier to sharpen than a stainless-steel knife. Stainless steel keeps a good edge when sharpened, though. As you get accustomed to lightly sharpening your knife every time you use it, the high-carbon steel will be your best bet.

- 8-inch Japanese vegetable knife (usuba) or 8-inch chef knife
- 12-inch serrated bread knife
- 1 paring knife
- 1 sharpening steel

Utensils

- 1 or 2 vegetable peelers: one should have the peeler part perpendicular to the handle (which makes it easier and faster to use on produce such as butternut squash)
- 8-inch bowl-shaped strainer (sieve)
- bamboo skewers
- colander for rinsing vegetables or draining pasta or cooked veggies
- cutting board: wood or plastic is fine. I like them about 16 x 12 inches and about ½ to ¾ inch thick. This size is easiest to handle and clean.
- funnel set
- ginger grater
- kitchen scissors, for opening packaging or trimming artichokes
- metal spatula
- mortar and pestle or suribachi, for grinding and mashing. The mortar and pestle is made of porcelain or wood, and the suribachi is usually made from clay and has ridges on the bottom of the bowl to help the grinding action.
- pastry brush (made of nylon, not animal bristles)
- pepper mill, for grinding your own, as store-bought ground pepper can be stale

- potato masher
- reamer, for quickly juicing a lemon or other citrus fruit
- rolling pin
- rubber spatula or "spoonula"
- spring-loaded tongs
- stainless-steel slotted spoon
- steaming basket, for cooking veggies
- timer
- vegetable brush, for scrubbing veggies
- wire whisk
- wooden spoon
- zester

Appliances

- toaster oven: great for quick reheats and toasting without having to heat the big oven.
- food processor, for those who don't want to chop by hand and for mixing.
- blender: I recommend Vita-Mix, a "high-performance" blender that enables you to do so many things (including grinding grains, kneading dough, and even cooking soup!). These blenders have a powerful motor and hold a larger capacity, and every little part is replaceable. They are a little expensive, but you will never have to buy another in your life.
- electric hand mixer
- electric rice cooker (for cooking all kinds of grains)

Storage

It's always best to store dry goods (such as grains and beans) in a cool and somewhat dark location unless you are using them right away.

- glass jars
- reusable plastic containers of various sizes

Extras

Here's a list of additional items you might want to get when you're feeling the cooking friskies.

- 10-inch cast-iron skillet
- 12-inch stainless steel skillet
- wok-style skillet
- stockpot
- pressure cooker: great for beans and grains. If you spring for one of these, you may end up cooking more frequently, because the cooking time is much reduced.
- 6-inch serrated knife
- a second paring knife
- countertop electric mixer with dough hook
- electric countertop deep fryer: good for frying tofu cubes
- mandoline slicer: a manual slicer that aids in rapid and uniform cutting of vegetables julienne, cutting french fries, and slicing thin.
- Benriner slicer: This Japanese vegetable slicer makes long, thin curls and other creative shapes that add some fun in garnishing and serving vegetables. It's a manual device, similar to the mandoline, and operates by rotating the vegetable against different blades.
- soy milk maker: it makes small amounts of tofu, too.
- cheesecloth, unbleached

PREPARATION AND COOKING

A Glossary of Cooking Terms

Most of the terms and styles of food preparation in this glossary are used in this book; I added a few extras that I thought would be useful or interesting. The glossary is for quick reference; for "how to," see the section "La Technique" on page 44.

à la A French idiom that means "in the style of." *À la maison* means in the style of the house, or house specialty.

al dente An Italian phrase that means "to the tooth," implying the cooking of pasta until tender but firm.

bake To cook in an oven with dry heat.

batter An uncooked mixture of flour, leavening, oil, and a liquid that is thin enough to pour.

beat To mix in a circular motion with a spoon, a whisk, or an electric beater.

blacken To coat a sautéed product (in this book it is either tempeh patties or soy brests) with a special spice mixture and sear it briefly on a hot griddle. See page 44 for directions.

blanch To submerge (vegetables) in boiling water briefly to loosen skins or cook slightly while retaining a bright color and fresh flavor.

blend To mix two or more ingredients together until smooth.

boil (1) To heat liquid until bubbles come to the surface and break. (2) To cook food in boiling water.

braise To brown in oil or fat, then to cook, covered, on the stovetop or in the oven with a little liquid.

brown To cook on the stovetop over high heat, usually in oil, until browned.

bruise	To partially crush, such as a garlic clove or a cardamom pod. Bruising can be done in a mortar and pestle or with the side of a large, flat knife.
Brunoise	(*broo-NWAHZ*) A French cooking term used to describe finely diced vegetables. See page 45.
brush	To apply an oil, a liquid, or a glaze with a brush.
café	French for "coffee."
caramelize	(1) To heat sugar until it melts and turns golden brown. (2) To slowly cook onions or other root vegetables until golden brown, thus releasing their natural sugars.
chiffonade	A garnish made by finely cutting strips, usually of lettuce, basil, or sorrel.
chop	To cut into small pieces. *Chopped* implies a coarser cut than *minced*.
clove of garlic	One segment of the garlic bulb.
combine	To mix two or more ingredients together.
cool	To allow hot food to come to room temperature.
core	To remove the core, as from apples.
cream	To beat a fat (such as nondairy margarine or shortening) alone or with other ingredients until soft and smooth.
crème	French for "cream."
crudité	Raw vegetables served as an appetizer with dipping sauce.
crumble	To break apart, using the fingers.
cut in	To mix shortening or other solid fat into dry ingredients, such as flour, until the texture is coarse and mealy. Cutting in is usually done with a fork or pastry cutter.
deep-fry	To immerse in hot oil kept at about 360°F and cook until golden brown and crispy.

deglaze	(1) To scrape off browned bits and flavors on the bottom of a pan or skillet by adding a small amount of liquid and heating, then using the flavored liquid. (2) The name of the sauce used for such a purpose. See recipe for Simple Deglaze on page 65.
dice	To cut into small cubes, usually about ⅛ to ¼ inch.
dilute	To thin by adding liquid.
dredge	To coat lightly with flour.
drizzle	To pour a liquid over a food in a fine stream; it can be done with a spoon or a squeeze bottle.
drop	To drop from a spoon; usually refers to dropping cookie dough onto a baking sheet.
entrée	(*AHN-tray*) The main course of a meal.
extract	A concentrated flavoring
flambé	(*flahm-BAY*) French for "flamed"; this dramatic method entails sprinkling a food with liquor and then setting it aflame.
flour	To coat with flour. Food may be floured, and so may oiled baking pans to prevent sticking.
flute	To make a decorative edge on a pie by crimping.
fold	To mix in a lighter or liquid ingredient into a heavier one, such as flour, by gently turning over and over with a spoon as to not overmix.
garnish	To decorate a dish before serving.

GARNISHES GALORE. You'll see a lot of chopped parsley and Brunoise-style chopped red bell pepper used in garnishing my dishes. That's because I always like to create a balanced color presentation. It's quick and easy to do, and it seems to be that extra touch that takes the dish over the edge.

When I worked with my father at large parties, at times we'd help the chef in the kitchen by garnishing plates. Chopped parsley was often used, and sometimes the tendency was to use a pinch or two, whereupon my father would instruct: "Never be afraid of parsley." Well, it stuck. It looks pretty—and it's a great source of chlorophyll, the substance in plants that harnesses the sun's energy in photosynthesis. It's like eating sunshine! Chlorophyll also freshens the breath.

....

glaze   To cover food with a shiny coating of syrup or melted jelly, or brush it with soy milk before baking to impart a glossy tone.

grease   To rub with fat or oil

grease and flour   To first grease a baking pan and then dust it lightly with flour to prevent sticking.

grill   To cook on a grill that uses wood or natural gas and lava rocks as a heat source. There are electric grills, but they don't impart any flavor as the others do. Charcoal briquettes are not recommended, as they are made from petroleum by-products and impart tar.

infuse   To extract a flavor from an ingredient by steeping it in a liquid (usually heated), such as tea in water or an herb in oil.

julienne   To cut food into matchstick strips. See page 47.

knead   To rhythmically work (a dough) with the hands in a pressing-folding-turning movement. Kneading may also be done by machine.

macrobiotics   A way of eating based on traditional Chinese and Japanese thought on the healing properties of foods. Originally introduced to the West by a Japanese man named George Ohsawa, the movement gained momentum in America through two of Ohsawa's students, Michio Kushi and Herman Aihara. A variety of whole grains are emphasized along with fresh vegetables, beans, sea vegetables, and condiments such as miso and tamari. The importance of seasonal, organic, and locally grown foods is stressed, as is eating foods grown in the climate zone in which one lives, as they are easier for the body to assimilate and provide better energetic qualities. Refined sweeteners are extremely discouraged. Much macrobiotic theory is based on the Taoist yin-yang theory of complementary opposites, and foods and body organs are classified as contractive (yang) or expansive (yin). The art is in eating foods that balance each other, thereby balancing body functions for optimal health. It's all about balance!

marinate To steep food in a liquid (usually containing a vinegar or acid base) for a period of time to allow flavors to permeate.

mince To chop into very small pieces. Mincing produces a finer result than chopping.

mix To stir in circular motion.

mocha A combination of coffee and chocolate flavors.

pickle To preserve in a vinegar or salty brine.

pipe To squirt through a pastry bag fitted with a tip, usually for decorative effects.

preheat To bring the oven to the required temperature before putting food in.

purée To grind to a paste by whirling in a blender or food mill.

reconstitute To rehydrate or restore liquid to a dried product.

reduce To boil (a liquid) down until the volume is reduced and the flavors are concentrated.

roast To cook uncovered in the oven by dry heat. See page 46.

roll out	To use a rolling pin on food (usually dough) to bring it to the desired degree of thinness.
sauté	(*saw-TAY*) To cook in a skillet with just enough oil so that all the oil is used in the cooking of the product.
sear	To cook quickly with high heat, using minimal amounts of oil and liquid. Searing browns the food and locks in flavor.
seed	To remove seeds.
set or set up	To let thicken, off heat, usually after having been heated.
sieve	(1) To strain liquid through a sieve. (2) The implement used for sieving.
sift	To put flour or other dry ingredients through a sieve. Sifting removes large pieces and adds air to the mixture, making it lighter and the final baked product fluffier.
simmer	(1) To heat liquid just until bubbles lightly form (about 185°F). (2) To cook food in simmering liquid.
skewer	To pierce and thread chunks of food on metal or bamboo pointed sticks, or skewers.
steam	To cook, covered, over boiling liquid so that the steam is what cooks the food.
steep	To let ingredients such as tea, spices, or herbs sit in hot liquid until their flavor is extracted. Same as *infuse*.
stir	To mix with a spoon or whisk in a circulating motion.
stir-fry	To sauté while quickly stirring and tossing foods; an Asian cookery style.
stock	The broth reserved from stewed vegetables, grains, or beans.
strain	To separate solids from liquid by pouring through a sieve.
toast	To cook with dry heat so that food becomes cooked to a light brown color, as when toasting seeds in a skillet (see page 48) or bread in a toaster.

whisk To stir or whip with a whisk, an implement made from looped wires.

zest To remove the zest, the colored part of the citrus rind, which contains the oil and flavor. See page 48.

La Technique: A Glossary of Preparation and Cooking Methods

Mastering these techniques will make you unique.

blackening

To blacken *tempeh patties*: Brush a little oil onto one side of each sautéed tempeh patty (see page 65). Place some of Ray's Good Home Blackening Spice (page 101) in a flat dish or plate, and press the oiled side gently into the spice to coat well. Allow a clean and dry cast-iron griddle or skillet to get very hot on the stovetop, and then place the spiced side down on the hot surface. Let it sear and smoke 5 or 10 seconds, until spice mixture "blackens." Then remove and serve.

To blacken *soy brests*: First reconstitute brests (page 76), marinate with Basic Marinade (page 76), and sauté. Place some of Ray's Good Home Blackening Spice (page 101) in a flat dish or plate. Brush one side of brest with a little oil, and press the oiled side gently into the spice to coat well. Allow a clean and dry cast-iron griddle or skillet to get very hot on the stovetop, and then place the spiced side down on the hot surface. Let it sear and smoke 5 or 10 seconds, until spice mixture "blackens." Then remove and serve.

blanching

Also known as parboiling, blanching is a method used for quickly cooking vegetables; if the vegetable is on the bitter side, it will remove some of the bitterness. It is done by bringing a pot of water to a boil, adding a couple of pinches of salt, and then boiling the vegetable until softened. Each vegetable varies in the amount of time needed, but it's never more than a few minutes. The pot should be uncovered, as this helps retain the color of the vegetable. Once cooked, the vegetable can be immediately placed under cold running water (a technique known as *shocking*) to stop the cooking and keep the color intact. The cooking water is great to reuse for soups and other dishes.

Brunoise	This technique comes from France, the source of many loving, artistic techniques. In this book I use the term to refer to finely cut small cubes for garnishing. I mostly do it with bell peppers, but it can be done with carrots or any vegetable with color if you are using the technique solely for garnishing.

To Brunoise-cut a bell pepper, first remove the ends and slice once lengthwise to open the bell pepper and expose its "panels." Cut these so that you end up with rectangular pieces. The white pithy part and seeds need to be removed, so that you end up with as flat a rectangle as possible to ensure nice, even squares. Slice each rectangle into even, thin slices lengthwise $\frac{1}{8}$ inch wide (julienne). Turn the slices and chop them in about $\frac{1}{8}$-inch slices slowly and evenly, ending up with tiny cubes.

chiffonade Used for leafy vegetables or herbs such as basil, this is a great technique for slicing delicate items. Basil, for example, will bruise and become black if chopped. Stack the individual leaves together. Roll them together from base to tip, then thinly slice the rolled leaves.

chopping If you are using a round vegetable such as an onion, it is best to cut it in half lengthwise and then, with the flat side on the cutting board, proceed to make horizontal $\frac{1}{4}$- to $\frac{1}{2}$-inch cuts not quite all the way through to the end. Then cut in $\frac{1}{4}$- to $\frac{1}{2}$-inch vertical slices, producing square-cut pieces.

If you are using long vegetables, like carrots or zucchini, slice them in half. Then slice halves lengthwise into $\frac{1}{4}$- to $\frac{1}{2}$-inch slices; then cut those slices in strips lengthwise and then across again.

Chopping implies less uniformity than other techniques, so if you're off a little, no big deal!

....

CUTTING BOARD HINT: Before beginning chopping, place a dampened paper towel or kitchen towel underneath. This will keep the board from sliding around while you are chopping, reducing the risk of slipping and possible injury.

....

dicing   Chopping in small, uniform cubes about 1/8 to 1/4 inch in size.

grating   There are a couple of different kinds of grating or shredding techniques, one of which used to be for grating dairy cheese (in the pre-vegan days). The other, often used for grating peeled ginger root, entails using a grater that has no holes in the back so that the fibrous part of the ginger stays and just the juice and flesh rub out.

mincing   Cutting into very fine, small pieces without a distinct pattern, so that the result is almost mashed. Mincing is often used in the preparation of garlic or ginger.

roasting   Cooking in the oven, in an uncovered pan, at higher temperatures than baking.

Roasting *vegetables* helps to sear flavors and achieve a crispier texture on the outside.

To roast *nuts or seeds,* spread them evenly on a baking pan or cookie sheet and place in a preheated oven at 350°F for 10–20 minutes, depending on the size and thickness of the nut or seed. Be sure to use a timer and check occasionally, because if you forget, you lose your nuts! *See also* toasting.

roll cutting   This technique is for long, thick vegetables like carrots or parsnip. Begin at the base and cut on a diagonal; then roll the item one quarter way around and do it again, and again, and again, until you've reached the top. I enjoy doing a roll cut; it's relaxing in a Zen sort of way. I liken the technique to trying to achieve a point when manually sharpening a pencil.

scaloppine	This Italian term usually refers to thin slices of meat created by pounding with a mallet, then sautéed. In this book, it simply means a thin slice of tempeh or seitan. See, for example, the directions for Tempeh Scaloppine (page 215).
shredding	It is done on the large holes of a standard grater or with a knife, cutting in ⅛-inch strips. Cabbage is often shredded, and you also shred romaine lettuce, for garnishing sandwiches.
slicing	Begin by first peeling the vegetable if necessary; then slice in whatever thickness the recipe calls for.

Half moons are slices made first by cutting the vegetable in half lengthwise and then slicing. The slices resemble half moons.

Diagonal slices are usually done with long vegetables like carrots or zucchini. Instead of straight rounds, you cut at an angle. This achieves an attractive appearance.

Julienne slices are of a long, thin matchstick size or thinner. Cut the vegetable first into diagonal or in rectangular shapes ⅛ inch in thickness, and then cut in strips. You can also use a vegetable peeler to make long, thick cuts; then roll the slices and cut them into strips.

To slice *garlic or shallots*, peel the skin from the individual cloves and thinly slice lengthwise.

....

FULL MOON COOKING: Once I held a Full Moon evening cooking class and instead of slicing in half moons we cut everything in whole slices and called them "full moons." We haven't revolutionized the cooking world with that one, but are working on it . . . at least once a month!

....

steaming	Begin by placing about 1½ to 2 inches of water in the bottom of a 2- or 3-quart saucepan, and then put a steamer basket into the pan. Bring the water to a boil and place vegetables inside the basket, putting in denser vegetables

(such as carrots) first, since they will take longer to cook. The steam will hit them first, allowing them to cook before other vegetables, and then the timing should be good for them all to be done at the same time. Lighter vegetables like zucchini and broccoli should be at the top. Cover the saucepan and steam about 10–12 minutes or less if you don't have dense veggies at the bottom. Do this regularly, and you'll get an intuitive feel for the timing—it's quite easy, really!

toasting To toast items such as sesame seeds and shredded coconut: Heat a small skillet over medium-high heat. Put the seeds in the pan, and shake or stir to keep them moving. When the aroma begins to rise, remove the pan from the heat and place the seeds in a flat container or on a plate to cool. *See also* roasting.

zesting This is a term used for removing the outer (colored) part of a fresh citrus fruit, also known as the rind, for flavoring. A citrus zester is an extremely handy implement to have, and the little strips of citrus that it makes are also useful as a decorative garnish. Another handy tool is a micro-plane zester, which grates the zest very fine and almost powder-like. If you have neither, use a vegetable peeler, taking care not to peel off too much of the bitter white pith along with the colored rind. Then thinly slice or chop the removed rind.

MEASURE FOR MEASURE

Using Measuring Cups and Spoons

Dry Ingredients

Flours should be spooned lightly into measuring cups. Do not tap or shake down the contents. Molasses sugar should be packed firmly when measuring.

Shortening should be packed a little at a time into a measuring cup and the air pockets pressed out.

When measuring *dry ingredients* in measuring spoons, scoop up the ingredients so that the spoon is overfilled; then run the flat edge of a knife across the top of the spoon so that excess ingredient is removed. If a "heaping" spoon is called for, do not remove the excess with a knife.

Liquids and Oils

- Fill liquids to the line on measuring cups, and view at eye level to be exact.
- Fill liquids to the top of a measuring spoon.

Pots and Pans

Square or rectangular baking pans are measured by length times width times depth, such as a 9 x 13 x 2–inch baking pan; or sometimes just length times width, such as an 8 x 8–inch square baking pan.

Round baking pans are measured by their diameter and are usually referred to as cake pans, such as an 8-inch or 9-inch round cake pan.

Stovetop pots are measured by volume, such as 1 quart, 2 quart, 3 quart, and larger. These are what we refer to in this book as *saucepans* or *soup pots*. A small saucepan would be a

1- or 2-quart. A medium saucepan would be a 3- or 4-quart; 5 quarts and up would be called a soup pot. Sometimes it says at the bottom of a pot what size it is; if not, you can find out by premeasuring water and recording how much it takes to fill the pot.

Stovetop pans are referred to as *skillets* in this book and are measured by their diameter, such as 6, 10, or 12 inches. They are sometimes referred to as small, medium, and large as well.

MEASURING EQUIVALENTS

pinch or dash	=	less than $\frac{1}{8}$ teaspoon
3 teaspoons	=	1 tablespoon
4 tablespoons	=	$\frac{1}{4}$ cup
1 cup	=	8 ounces
2 cups	=	1 pint
4 cups	=	1 quart
4 quarts	=	1 gallon
16 ounces	=	1 pound
8 ounces	=	$\frac{1}{2}$ pound
4 ounces	=	$\frac{1}{4}$ pound

basic beanery

When you think of beans, are you reminded of the arts and crafts you created in kindergarten or the items in preschool that helped you learn to count? It's too bad we never learned about eating them! Well, it's never to late to learn, and once you learn, it's hard to unlearn.

Beans and other legumes (such as dried peas and lentils) come second only to grains as the most nutritional food used worldwide for human subsistence. They can be eaten in different stages of their existence. Some are eaten green, either in and with their pod, such as green beans or snow peas, or shelled and eaten without their pod, such as fava beans, green peas, and fresh soybeans (edamame). The majority of beans, and those we are most familiar with, are of the dried variety, which can be stored for long periods of time. These need to be soaked and boiled before they are eaten. Pinto beans, black beans, and garbanzo beans are examples of this type.

Make a fresh pot of beans every few days, and you'll always have some at hand for a quick, low-fat, high-quality, nutritious meal or snack!

KNOW YOUR BEANS

Below is a list of some bean favorites There are many more specialty and heirloom (ancient species) beans. Check the market shelves and specialty stores, and learn to recognize the varieties.

Adzuki—also spelled *azuki* (*a-ZOO-kee*)—are small red beans with a sweet and nutty flavor and a firm texture. They are prized in Japan, where they are cooked in both savory and sweet dishes, including a sweetened purée used as a filling or topping. In the macrobiotic world they are a preferred bean for eating regularly, as they contain less fat or oil than other beans. COOKING TIME: 1 hour.

Black beans, native to South America, are also used widely in Central America, Cuba, Puerto Rico, the Caribbean, and Spain. They are sometimes called *black turtle* beans. COOKING TIME: 1–1 1/2 hours.

Black-eyed peas are said to be a Chinese relative of the mung bean. They found their way to India and Africa and because of the slave trade ended up in America, where they became a staple of Southern cooking. They have a light and smooth texture. COOKING TIME: 1 hour.

Garbanzo beans (*chickpeas*) have a great nutty flavor and a firm texture. They are the most widely grown bean in India, where they are known as *channa dal* and also ground into flour (called *besan* or "gram flour") for making flat breads. The Middle East made this bean famous in a dish called *hummus*. They are extremely popular in Greek cuisine. Most garbanzos have a yellowish color, but there is a variety called *Black Kabuli* that is quite nice and makes a cool-looking black hummus. COOKING TIME: 2–2 1/2 hours.

Kidney beans, indigenous to Mexico, are usually a deep dark red color. They have a meaty texture and are commonly used in chili recipes. Other varieties are *red beans*, a smaller version of kidney beans, and cannelli beans, white Italian kidney beans. COOKING TIME: 1–1 1/2 hours.

Lentils originated in southwest Asia. The most popular in the United States are brown lentils and green lentils (the green is an olive color). *French lentils* are a variety of green lentil with a tortoiseshell appearance. *Puy* green lentils are grown in a special small area in France called Le Puy and must be grown according to French regulations that ensure their quality. *Red lentils* are beautiful orange color and are very soft when cooked. The smaller *masoor* lentils you see at Indian markets are either the brown or the orange masoor. The brown masoor are the orange masoor with their seed coats on. They take a little longer to cook then regular brown lentils. COOKING TIMES: brown and green lentils, 45 minutes; red lentils, 20 minutes.

Lima beans and **baby lima** beans taste about the same, the larger being meatier. Native to Central America, these beans eventually reached Peru and were named after its capital city. In North America, the Algonquin Indians made a dish called succotash with corn and lima beans. COOKING TIME: 1½–2 hours.

Mung beans are beady little olive green legumes that cook quickly. They are very popular in East Indian spiced lentil dishes (*dals*). (Many Indian cookbooks call for the split yellow mung without the skins. This quick-cooking dal is available in Indian groceries.) When you buy fresh bean sprouts loose at the market, these are the beans they were sprouted from. COOKING TIME: for whole mung: 45 minutes–1 hour.

Pinto beans, reddish brown with lighter streaks, are *muy popular* in Mexican cuisine, and when cooked and mashed are delicious as *refritos*, or refried beans. COOKING TIME: 1½–2 hours.

Soybeans, the Queen of Beans, contain 35 to 38 percent protein and all the essential amino acids that the body doesn't manufacture on its own. They've been cultivated for over five thousand years and have served as the major source of protein for the people of China, Japan, Korea, and Indonesia. Europe has had them for about three hundred years, while the United States began using them in the 1900s and is currently the world's largest producer, at over 50 metric tons per year, or about 500 pounds per citizen. Most of these soybeans are fed to factory farm animals. In the Midwest soybeans are also known as sweet beans. Edamame are soybeans eaten green out of the pod, roasted and seasoned, or boiled for stews or healing teas. (See page 135 in the "Snacks 'n' Apps" chapter.) Most dried soybeans are a yellowish color, one exception being the black soybean. COOKING TIME FOR DRIED SOYBEANS: 2–2½ hours.

....

PRAISE SOYBEANS! Soybeans are made into delicious food products such as dairy alternatives, miso, tempeh, tofu, soy sauce, and the various styles of textured soy protein and soy protein isolates. Let's not forget the use of soy oil for cooking and the lecithin derived from the processing of the beans. A mixture of fatty substances, lecithin is indispensable to many food products, including chocolate, to which it imparts texture and chewiness.

All of the traditional soy products, including tofu, soy milk, tempeh, and miso, as well as soybeans themselves (but not soy sauce or soy oil), have high concentrations of isoflavones, plant-based estrogens that provide many disease-preventing health benefits for both men and women. Have you had your isoflavones today?

....

A PROPHET OF SOY: The automobile pioneer Henry Ford was also a visionary promoter of soybeans who hosted events where he would serve all soy foods known at the time, including soy milk, nuts, and crackers. He experimented with running some of his compressors with soy oil and even made a car with plastic parts made of soy and other crops.

Corvette and Avanti took off on that idea and went on to make vehicles with synthetic plastics instead of soy-based ones. Ford even made a wool-like fiber out of soy and hoped that World War II military uniforms would be made with it.

Ford passed away after the war, and his chemist went to work for Hormel. It was there he developed a textured soy protein called bacon bits. Further soy food science was not investigated at the time, owing to the rebuilding of the beef industry from the slump in the economy after the war.

....

Split peas come in green and yellow varieties. The fresh peas have been allowed to dry, which gives them a sweeter essence. Split peas make a yummy, hearty soup. COOKING TIME: 40–50 minutes.

White beans include four types: *great northern beans*, *navy beans*, *pea beans*, and the big *marrowfat*. COOKING TIME: 1½–2 hours.

HOW TO COOK BEANS

If you are following a recipe that includes beans, do as it says. If you just want to cook a pot of beans, here's a general guideline:

Pick the amount you'd like to cook. Most beans double in volume from dry to cooked. One cup of dried beans serves about four people. Soybeans and garbanzo beans usually triple, so you are going to have a little extra here.

Sort through the beans to look for tiny stones and broken beans. It's better to take a minute here and look than wait until you or your dinner guests find a piece of something with their tooth.

Rinse beans by running cool, clear water over them in a colander or sieve.

Soak beans in water. For every cup of beans, soak in 4 cups of water. Soaking time varies; 6 hours is usually good for most. Overnight is convenient, so just soak your beans before you go to bed.

Draining the beans before you cook them in fresh water apparently helps eliminate some of the flatulence they may create. There is also the controversy that by doing so the vitamins are lost, but apparently this loss is negligible. I don't like to drain the soak water from black beans, as it takes away their color.

After soaking and draining, put beans in a saucepan and cover with 2 inches of water. Add a 1-inch strip of rinsed kombu for every cup of dry beans to be cooked. This increases the nutritional content of the beans and also helps their digestibility.

Bring to a boil and and then lower heat and simmer, partially covered, for the determined time mentioned for each bean variety.

Do not salt until the last 10 minutes of cooking or the beans will not cook. Use ½ tsp for each cup of dried beans, adding more or less to your taste.

BEAN YIELDS

2 cups dry beans = 1 pound
1 cup dry beans   = 2–3 cups cooked
1 cup dry beans   = 4 servings

....

BEANS COOKING TIP: If you add salt at the beginning of cooking beans, they will never get soft. Here's the reason why: Water enters the bean during cooking through a small pore. The size of a salt molecule is larger than the size of a water molecule, so if the salt enters first, it will block the pore and not allow water to enter. So add your salt and seasonings during the last few minutes of cooking.

....

grains for brains

Grains are the seeds of grass. When humans learned that this great food source could be planted to provide food for many, an evolution of the mind occurred where it was no longer necessary to kill in order to survive—an idea many of our species are still trying to communicate to one another!

Grains supply the most nutrition for most of the world's human population. They add great texture and creativity to meals. The grains we are most familiar with are wheat, rice, and corn. Other, less familiar grains that we may have heard of include barley, millet, spelt, and quinoa. I suggest cooking at least one new grain a month. This will build your grain "inventory" and add grains to your diet more regularly, keeping things innovative and exciting. Stronger body, stronger mind—grains for brains!

amaranth Amaranth is not a true cereal grass but a weedy plant of the pigweed family, indigenous to Central and South America, and also to India and Nepal. The seed is high in protein and about the size of a poppy seed. The leaves of amaranth are also eaten as well, but I haven't tried them . . . yet. The blooms produced by the plant are unique and beautiful, with colors of purple, orange, red, or gold.

....

ADD A LITTLE AMARANTH: Since it is such a small grain, I like to add a tablespoon or two of amaranth when cooking my other grains. There is no need to increase the water measurement of the grain I add it to. I also like to toss a couple of tablespoons into a soup when cooking, for some added protein and texture.

••

barley Barley has been cultivated for thousands of years. The ancients regarded it as a strength builder. For example, it's said that ancient Greek boats that traveled long voyages through rough seas were manned by rowers fed on olive oil and barley. (Maybe this is where the terms "Adonis" and "six-pack" arose!) *Pearl barley* is the polished grain, also known as Job's tears. *Scotch barley*, a more nutritious variety since it is not milled, is husked and coarsely ground. *Heirloom black barley* is also available from specialty markets or suppliers. *Roasted barley* makes a tasty, healthful unsweetened tea, enjoyed hot or cold. It is very popular in Japan where it is sold canned and bottled.

buckwheat Buckwheat is a cereal unrelated to wheat. Siberian in origin, it is used in many Russian recipes. After it has been cooked and prepared pilaf-style, it is called *kasha*.

corn A native of the Americas, corn is commonly seen in white, yellow, and blue varieties. A larger species known as *white flint corn* is commonly known as *hominy* in the South and used in *posole*, a delicious soup, in Mexico. *Polenta* is cooked cornmeal. And what would life be like without popcorn?

groats This term indicates a grain that has been coarsely ground or cracked, usually buckwheat.

millet Many Americans think of millet as bird food, but to most cultures in the Near East and Africa it has been a staple for thousands of years, and there are many different species. It resembles couscous when cooked but is a whole grain, high in iron and quick-cooking.

oats When the oat grain is mechanically pressed or rolled, we commonly know this grain as *oatmeal*. It can be ground as well.

quinoa (*KEEN-wah*) This ancient grain (not a true grass but related to the same family as beets, spinach, and chard) was held sacred by the Incas. It is a small, quick-cooking grain rich in high-quality protein, with an almost completely balanced amino acid composition. When cooked, it has a light, fluffy texture.

rice There are hundreds of varieties of rice, ranging from the Bhutanese red to the tiny grains of kalijira from Bangladesh. There is black rice as well as brown rice. Brown rice is of course the whole rice kernel with its bran intact, and unlike white rice it retains most of its B vitamins and vitamin E. It is chewier and heartier than white rice. The two most commonly available varieties of brown rice are long-grain and short-grain. Short-grain needs about ½ cup more water and 15 more minutes cooking time (per 1 cup dry) and has a chewier, heavier texture than the long-grain brown rice. *Sweet brown rice* is a short-grain species with greater sugar content, thereby making it sticky after cooking. It is very hearty, chewy, and fun for an occasional change.

The white rices have been milled and polished, and are thus less nutritious than brown rice but are valued for their light texture. Basmati and jasmine rice are becoming increasingly easier to find in brown versions, with their seed coat intact. *Basmati* grows in India at the base of the Himalayas and has a distinct delightfully dense aroma. Attempts to grow it outside its native habitat never seem to elicit the aroma and flavor of the Indian rice. *Jasmine* rice is a species of basmati rice grown in Thailand.

Converted rice is polished and parboiled, and *quick* rice is fully cooked and dehydrated rice. These processed types should be avoided. I always stock long-grain and short-grain brown rice and sweet brown rice in my pantry.

See also wild rice.

rye   Mostly grown for use in flour and whiskey, rye is sometimes found as rye groats. It has a deeper flavor than most other grains.

spelt   A more ancient and less domesticated species of wheat, spelt can be tolerated by some people who are allergic to wheat.

wheat   The staff of life for much of the world. There are numerous different species with different qualities. Wheat is ground for flours, or cracked and known as *bulgur* wheat, which is used in Middle Eastern dishes such as tabouli. *Semolina* flour, from the heart of durum wheat, and is used for the highest-quality and best-textured pasta. Ground into granules, it is the source of *farina* or *couscous* (see page 20). Of course, *seitan* is made from the staff of life as well!

wheat berries   The whole kernels of wheat, which can be sprouted into wheat grass or cooked and eaten like rice.

wild rice   This delicacy is not actually in the rice family, though it is cooked similarly; it is the long, slender seed of an aquatic grass native to the northern Great Lakes region of the United States.

Basic Grain Cookery

The size of the grain is basically what determines its cooking times and the amount of water used; thus cracked or ground grains take less time than whole grains. The accompanying table is a general guide. Always follow package instructions, as the manufacturers know their product best.

For cooking 1 cup of grains, a 2-quart saucepan is fine. If you are cooking larger portions, use an appropriately larger-sized pot.

In addition to the water, I like to add a 1-inch strip of kombu seaweed that has been rinsed, and a pinch of salt. You can use the kombu alone and eliminate the salt if you'd like, and use condiments (such as Gomasio, page 95) at the table to season your grain. Adding kombu to a grain when cooking gives the grain a nice mineral and vitamin boost. The molecular size of the mineral is smaller than the water molecule, so they zoom in nicely as the water fills the grain. Some of the kombu dissolves, and sometimes a piece is left; you may remove and discard it or chop it and incorporate it into the rice, as it is completely edible.

• •

Measure 1 cup of grain of choice. Rinse by placing in sieve and running under cool clear water. While rinsing, check for stones or other debris. See the accompanying table for the ratio of water to grains and the cooking instructions. (If using pressure cooker, reduce water by ½ cup and reduce cooking time by half.)

GRAINS	MEASUREMENT	DIRECTIONS
amaranth (30 min.) basmati rice (20 min.) buckwheat groats (20 min.) cracked wheat or bulghur (10–15 min.) jasmine rice (20 min.) millet (20 min.) rolled oats (20 min.)	1 cup grain to 2 cups water	Bring to boil, reduce heat, cover, and simmer for the time indicated for each grain.
long-grain brown rice (40 min.) short-grain brown rice (50–55 min.)	1 cup grain to 2½ cups water 1 cup grain to 3 cups water	Bring to boil, reduce heat, cover, and simmer for the time indicated.
teff (20 min.)		
barley spelt wheat berries	1 cup grain to 3 cups water	Bring to boil, reduce heat, cover, and simmer for 1½ hours. Presoaking these grains will reduce the cooking time.
quinoa	1 cup grain to 2 cups water	Rinse in strainer under running water for a minute or two to remove bitterness. Bring to boil, reduce heat, cover, and simmer for 10–15 minutes.
cornmeal grits	1 cup grain to 5 cups water	Bring to boil, reduce heat, and continue to cook, uncovered, stirring frequently, for 40 minutes. The time can vary depending on how fine or coarse the texture is. You may have to adjust by increasing the cooking time and possibly adding more water. (Omit the kombu if you like, as it will be a little clumpy-looking.)

tempeh

Food of the Gods and Goddesses

*T*empeh (*TEM-pay*) is a soy food with culture in more ways than one. It originated in the culturally rich tropical paradise of Indonesia hundreds of years ago, where it continues to be popular. It is rapidly increasing in popularity in the United States, where it was first introduced in the 1950s, though it wasn't until around 1975 that it really took off, along with the new interest in natural foods and vegetarianism. Tempeh is also popular in Holland, since Indonesia was a Dutch colony from the late 1600s until 1949.

The method of making tempeh is simple; the longest part is the incubation time, where you basically wait and do nothing for 24 hours, except maybe soak some beans for the next batch—or catch a wave if in Indonesia! Dried soybeans are soaked, then cracked and boiled. They can be used alone, but it is common to mix them with a cooked grain, such as rice. In Indonesia coconut or "peanut press cake" (the leftovers after extracting peanut oil) are used as well as other legumes.

Then a culture is added, also known as a *starter*, similar to those used in making dairy cheese, yogurt, bread, and miso. The culturing process is also called "fermentation," but I dislike calling it that, since people often have a negative reaction to that word. It seems to make it sound "yucky" in contrast to the truly "yummy" food it creates! The soybean mixture is then put in trays (banana leaves in Indonesia) and kept at a warm temperature (82°–92°F) and in an extremely clean environment and left for 24 hours. What happens during

A 3.5-ounce serving of tempeh contains 160 calories, 6 grams fat, 19 grams protein, 11.3 grams carbohydrate, and 6.9 milligrams iron. Plus fiber! Isoflavones!

this period is the magic. The culture grows throughout the soybean mixture, forming a threadlike structure called the mycellium, which eventually makes the loose grains and soybeans turn into a solid cake that can be sliced, sautéed, and made into one of our fabulous Bali Burgers!

The culturing process also makes the soybeans more digestible. Tempeh is high in protein and iron, especially Native Foods' tempeh because we use millet in our recipe. It is a whole, nonprocessed food; has soluble and insoluble fiber, which have been found to be cholesterol-reducing; and is cholesterol-free. With its mild flavor and delicate texture, tempeh lends itself to simple meals like burgers and stir-frys or elegant gourmet presentations like Tempeh Scaloppine with Wild Mushroom Sauce and Tempeh Provençale (see "Entrées").

Fresh tempeh is the best! At the moment I took my first bite of homemade tempeh, I knew this was the "in" for food service in achieving a texture and flavor that would take vegetarian menus beyond Pasta Primavera, steamed veggies, and bean and rice burritos. If you'd like to try your hand at making it, contact G.E.M. Cultures in Northern California (www.gemcultures.com; 707-964-2922) and ask for their tempeh starter kit. The Farm in Summertown, Tennesee (www. healthy-eating.com), sells the starter as well as other soy alternatives, books, and more. You can link to them via our web site at www.nativefoods.com (click on "Shopping").

The following is my favorite quick and easy way to prepare tempeh. It can be baked and fried, as you will see in other recipes, but some of the recipes will call for the tempeh as shown below.

Tempeh Basic Prep

If you are buying commercial tempeh, you are going to get it in 8-ounce blocks. (I'm referring to the plain tempeh, not anything already prepared or marinated.) I suggest slicing the block in half lengthwise and then again in half crosswise to get four square patties about 2 ounces each.

VARIATIONS
• *Use Seitan Broth (page 70) instead of Simple Deglaze.*
• *If you are in a hurry or don't have any ginger or garlic, just use the water and soy sauce.*

3 Tbsp olive or sunflower oil

four 2- or 3-oz tempeh patties

¼ cup Simple Deglaze (recipe follows)

....

Heat oil in frying pan over moderately high heat. Add tempeh patties. They should sizzle slightly; that tells you oil is hot enough. (If the oil is too cool, you'll end up using more oil than you need to, as the patties will absorb more oil before they get brown.) Sauté until golden, about 1–2 minutes, then turn over and let other side brown. Here is where you may feel you need to add a little more oil to get the second side brown.

After the second side is brown and there is no excess oil in the pan, pour the Simple Deglaze over and around the tempeh patties all at once. This will make a sizzling sound.

Lower the flame slightly. Remove tempeh when the Simple Deglaze has been absorbed and the tempeh has a nice golden brown color.

Simple Deglaze

⅔ cup water

⅓ cup soy sauce

1 clove garlic, minced (or juice from pressing the garlic)

½ tsp grated fresh ginger

seitan

The Protein of Wheat

Seitan is a wonderful meatlike food dating back to China and the Near East over two thousand years ago. It is made by extracting the proteins (glutenin and gliadin) from wheat flour by kneading. For our restaurants, we make seitan in 2½-pound loaves, or "roasts," as we call them. Our Philly Peppersteak sandwich (page 194) is made from seitan. Boy, does that sandwich turn a lot of meat-lovers on to vegetarianism!

The name *seitan* is of Japanese origin, although after living in Japan I can tell you that very few people there knew of this ancient food source. It seems to have stopped being made after World War II, and the last few generations lost touch with it. Some of the older people who did know of it pronounced it *SOO-ee-tahn*, almost like *SWEET-ahn*. Here in the States we pronounce it *SAY-tan*.

Some folks get nervous about the Western pronunciation, because it seems to evoke the devil! One company that sells seitan once tried to make a positive play on words in their ad campaign, cleverly describing it as "devilishly good." We spent one summer selling our seitan roasts at the Malibu Farmers' Market, where we had great success. However, one day a woman came up for a sample, and as she was putting it in her mouth she asked what it was. When I answered, "Sei-tan," she immediately removed it from her mouth and said, "No, thank you, I believe in Jesus Christ!" I spent some time convincing her it was OK and it was really a wholesome food from wheat, the staff of life. She felt reassured and came back the next week for more samples.

To describe more about the process of seitan, let's remember that a wheat kernel contains both protein and starch (carbohydrate). Grinding the wheat kernels produces wheat flour. To begin seitan production, the flour is mixed with water and kneaded into a dough. The kneading binds the proteins enabling them to stick tightly together. The dough mass then rests for about 20 minutes, allowing the protein structures to develop.

The kneading then begins again but this time with water and in a bowl. This is actually the rinsing process, where it feels as if the whole thing is washing away in a swirling pool of cloudy water. What's happening here is that the starch portion of the wheat flour is separating from the protein. Starch is water-soluble, but the proteins are not.

What remains is a "stretchy-pully," elastic mass of protein, commonly known as gluten. It can be stretched, rolled, or pulled apart into balls. At this point it is still called *gluten*.

From here it is shaped and placed into a stockpot filled with a broth containing soy sauce and seasonings (see Seitan Broth, page 70) and slowly simmers for 2 hours. During this time it expands and becomes firm. It is when the simmering is finished that the mass officially makes the switch from just good old gluten to savory seitan.

The type of wheat flour used to make seitan will affect its quality. Generally you would want to use wheat that has a higher percentage of protein content. Sometimes it is difficult to tell when you are purchasing flour, but a wheat termed "hard" has a greater protein content than wheat termed "soft"; or look for a "high-gluten" flour. Each brand may vary slightly as well.

Combining flours in different ratios will give you different textures of seitan. I like to add a little pure gluten flour,

A 4-ounce serving of seitan has 130 calories, 1 gram fat, 20 grams protein, 0 carbohydrates, and 3.6 milligrams iron.

or vital gluten flour, for texture. This flour has already had the carbohydrate removed and is only the protein portion. Used alone, it is much too tough. The variations are endless, but here is a recipe to start with that I enjoy.

Roll up your sleeves and have some fun! Remember to turn on some good music!

(Commercially available seitan mixes do exist; try The Farm's Mail Order Catalog at www.healthy-eating.com.)

Makin' Seitan

I learned how to make seitan from my housemate, Joanie Anderson, while attending UC Santa Cruz. Not everything important was learned in the classroom. (See, Mom and Dad, I told you so!)

1 recipe Seitan Broth (recipe follows)
4 cups unbleached flour
1 cup whole wheat flour
1 cup gluten flour (see page 22)
2–2½ cups water

....

Begin to simmer Seitan Broth.

In a mixing bowl, combine flours well. Begin adding water slowly and consistently while stirring to form a well in the center. (Water absorption will slightly vary depending on the flours and your climate.) Incorporate dry flour from the outer circumference of the bowl toward the center of the well. Continue mixing until a firm dough is formed.

Dust a flat, firm work surface with unbleached flour and knead about 70 times; more is better. You will probably need to dust the dough with more flour if it gets slightly sticky to work with. (Did you remember to turn some good music on?)

Let it (and yourself) rest 20 minutes.

With the dough ball in the bowl, place the bowl in the sink and add water to cover the dough. Begin kneading the dough until the water turns really milky. Drain the water, add more fresh water, and repeat kneading process 10–12 times. (You could keep rinsing until the water becomes really clear, but I find that rinsing 10–12 times is fine.)

The following spice bases can be mixed together in a small bowl and then incorporated into the gluten (by kneading) after the last rinse and to give additional flavor styles.

• *Greek: 1 tablespoon olive or sunflower oil, 1 cup pitted and chopped Kalamata olives, 1 tablespoon dried oregano, ½ teaspoon garlic powder, ½ teaspoon sea salt.*

• *Italian Sausage: 1 tablespoon olive or sunflower oil, 1 tablespoon fennel seeds, 1 teaspoon dried thyme, ½ teaspoon dried oregano, ½ teaspoon garlic powder, ½ teaspoon onion powder, ½ teaspoon sea salt.*

• *Peppercorn: 1 tablespoon olive or sunflower oil, 1 tablespoon ground multicolored peppercorns, ½ teaspoon garlic powder, ½ teaspoon onion powder, ½ teaspoon sea salt.*

Form the gluten into shapes of your choice. If making a single loaf, pierce and weave a 12-inch bamboo skewer through it to hold it together, or you can wrap and tie with cheesecloth to hold more formed shape.

Gently place loaf in the simmering Seitan Broth, bring it to boil, then reduce to simmer again and cook 1½ hours. Remove from the pot and place on a plate to cool. Seitan will keep in the refrigerator for 3 weeks and stay frozen forever, but it probably won't last that long either way, since you'll want to eat it!

Seitan Broth

10 cups water

2 cups soy sauce

8 cloves whole garlic, peeled

4 bay leaves

three 2-inch slices fresh ginger

....

Place all ingredients in stockpot and bring to simmer.

1. Flours readied in mixing bowl.

2. Mixing in the water.

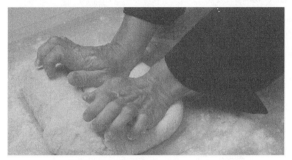

3. Kneading the dough.

4. Dough covered with water and ready to knead in the water.

5. Kneading and rinsing the dough in water.

6. Rinsed dough (gluten), skewered and ready to be simmered in broth.

7. Seitan fresh out of the pot after simmering.

Photographer: David Glomb
Food Styling: Brian Bergstrom

soy protein textures

Whaddaya Mean It's Not Meat?

REDEFINING MEAT

In the *Merriam-Webster Dictionary,* the first definition of meat is given as "solid food as distinguished from drink." So I think the new paradigm for the definition of meat should assume vegetarian "meat" rather than animal meat. Are you with me?

What I call soy protein textures are known in the soy foods industry as Textured Soy Protein (TSP) or Textured Vegetable Protein (TVP, a trademark of Archer Daniels Midland Co.), but I often refer to them by a generic term. These are dried soy products that, when rehydrated, have a meatlike texture, making them an ideal base for meals that satisfy those who are transitioning from a meat-centered diet.

This is the foodstuff that puts the "Mad" at the beginning of our Mad Cowboy recipe (page 227). It drives the wild men of the West crazy to believe, after they take the first bite, that what they are eating has nothing to do with Rocky Mountain Oysters. It isn't associated with the old "Home on the Range," but with the modern "home range." Giddyap, boys; this may be the tastiest food you've ever eaten!

Most vegans and vegetarians consider TSP a fun food for sure, while some think it's a little too processed (preferring whole foods) and dislike its resemblance to animal flesh. But it's great as a party food for both meat-lovers and veg-heads. This is a win, win situation, and so let the fun begin!

Soybeans are about 35 percent protein. The process of making soy protein textures starts with defatting (removing the oil from) soybeans and then grinding them into a flour or meal, now 50 percent protein. A soybean protein concentrate is then created by removing sucrose and soluble carbohydrates from the defatted soybean meal, and 70 percent protein content is obtained. From here, the use of extrusion cookers and adjustments of the extruder nozzles and of cutter speeds allows a variety of sizes and meaty textures to be produced. Double extrusion processing produces layered structures that are even closer to the texture of animal meats.

Initially (forty years ago) there were two reasons for making textured soy proteins. One was to use small amounts as food additives to improve production processes and quality and to lengthen product shelf-life; the other was to use them as extenders of meat products. Famous fast-food chain operations were the biggest purchasers for use as filler in their burgers. Why they didn't just eliminate the middle cow is beyond me!

This cookbook uses the textured soy protein products called granules, bits, flakes, chunks, and "brests." Which of these can you most readily buy today at the market? Most likely the granules, bits, or flakes, found at natural food markets or possibly the health food sections of supermarkets. Don't look for them at the 7-Eleven . . . yet.

The chunks and brests I refer to most likely will have to be purchased by mail order, but some markets with greater inventory selection may carry them in their bulk section. You can order these and the granules, bits, and flakes and other styles from The Mail Order Catalog for Healthy Eating in Summertown, Tennessee (www.healthy-eating.com). The granules and bits are organic as well and all are non-GMO (genetically modified organism). What would we have done without those fine folks for all these years? Send them thank-you notes! You can link to their site directly through our web site (www.nativefoods.com). Order up and get cooking!

Reconstitution for Granules, Bits, or Flakes

  1 cup textured soy protein granules, bits, or flakes

  1 cup water

....

Place ingredients in saucepan and bring to a boil. Remove from flame, cover, and let sit 10 minutes.

Taco Meat

  1 cup textured soy protein granules, bits, or flakes

  1 cup water

  1/4 cup soy sauce

  2 Tbsp olive oil

  1 tsp cumin powder

  1 tsp ground coriander

  1/4 tsp garlic powder

  1/4 tsp onion powder

  1/4 tsp crushed red chilies (optional)

....

Place ingredients in a saucepan and bring to a boil. Remove from flame, cover, and let sit 10 minutes.

Italian Ground Around

    1 cup soy bits or flakes

    1 cup water

    ¼ cup soy sauce

    2 Tbsp olive oil

    ½ tsp dried oregano

    1 tsp dried basil

    ¼ tsp garlic powder

    ¼ tsp onion powder

....

Place ingredients in a saucepan and bring to a boil. Remove from flame, cover, and let sit 10 minutes.

The following preparation for soy chunks and brests requires a marinade to give them a good base flavor, as they are thicker and denser than bits or flakes. They do not have much flavor on their own other than a cereal-like taste, so it's important to give them a good base flavor that can carry into other applications.

Reconstitution for Soy Chunks

    1 cup soy chunks

    1¼ cups water

....

Place ingredients in a saucepan, bring to a boil, then reduce heat and simmer 2–3 minutes. Remove from flame, cover, and let sit 10 minutes.

Reconstitution for Soy Brests

6–8 soy brests (sizes may vary)

4 cups water

....

Place ingredients in a saucepan, bring to a boil, then reduce heat and simmer, covered, 20–25 minutes.

$2\frac{1}{2}$ CUPS

Use this for marinating the reconstituted chunks and brests.

Basic Marinade

$1\frac{1}{2}$ cups water

$\frac{1}{2}$ cup soy sauce

$\frac{1}{4}$ cup lemon juice

....

Combine ingredients in a bowl and add chunks or brests. Chunks should marinate at least 30 minutes and brests at least 1 hour to overnight.

This is one basic style for preparing the brests that creates a nicely finished product. A little extra oil is used when sautéing them, since there is no oil or fat in the product itself, and it will help keep from sticking. Oil is not easily absorbed inside the brests either, so it stays mainly on the outside and helps brown and add flavor.

Sautéed and Grilled Brests

4–6 soy brests marinated in Basic Marinade

¼ cup olive, safflower, or sunflower oil

• •

To sauté the brests, heat the oil in a skillet and add the brests, making sure most of the marinade liquid is drained so that the oil does not splatter. Brown on both sides.

To grill the brests, brush both sides well with oil, place on a hot grill, and grill both sides.

how do you do tofu?

*T*ofu is a wonderful food that, like most of our modern-day soy products, was invented in Asia. It dates back to China over two thousand years and in Japan over one thousand years.

Tofu has been around long enough in this country to get a lot of attention, both negative and positive. I've heard everything from a disgusted "Eeeyew, tofu" to an enthusiastic "Yum!" There are bumper stickers that say "Tofu—The Other White Meat," and it's been called The Meat from the East and Poor Man's Chicken. I sometimes call it Poor Chicken's Defense!

Like most ancient soy foods, making tofu is a simple process. Soybeans are first soaked and then finely ground. This mixture is next boiled and simmered in water. When the water becomes a milky color, it is strained from the ground soybeans. The milky liquid is soy milk!

At this point a salt (not sodium) is added. A salt is essentially a naturally occurring positively charged mineral (sodium is just one kind). The mineral compounds mostly used are calcium sulfate and magnesium sulfate. The sea-derived nigari is also used, which is basically sea water with the sodium removed so as to leave other mineral salts, magnesium being the most prominent.

Once the calcium or magnesium sulfate or nigari is added, coagulation occurs, much as when rennet or enzymes are added to dairy milk to make cheese. Solids are formed and are strained from the liquid ("curds and whey" in dairy-speak). The solids or curd portion formed is tofu. It is then weighted and strained to condense the soft, malleable curds. Traditionally tofu is stored and sold in a water bath, but with today's technology you also find it in vacuum packaging without water. This "style" is called Chinese.

There are two different styles of tofu, the *Chinese* and the *silken* style. Silken tofu has a silky-soft, custardlike texture, achieved in the manufacturing process by not straining. In this style the solids and the liquid are never separated but gracefully mixed and allowed to firm up without being pressed. You will see silken-style tofu sold in aseptic box packaging as well as in a water bath. Since silken doesn't require straining the soy milk once the coagulant is added, it can be made right "in the box." The oxygen is removed in the aseptic packaging procedure, thereby making the shelf-life practically forever.

Both Chinese and silken styles are labeled according to their textures as well: soft, medium, firm, or extra firm. This is indicative of the amount of coagulant used to produce a more or less firm tofu regardless of its style. Each company has its own recipe, so be aware that each brand will vary with respect to these labeling textures.

Silken tofu lends itself well to puddings, bakery products, and other desserts. The Japanese serve it uncooked in summer, as it has a cooling quality. In the winter months they eat it warmed. One of my fondest food memories of Japan is *age dashi doufu*, which is silken tofu dusted with rice flour, deep fried, and served in a delicious soy sauce broth with freshly grated daikon, ginger, and green onions. As they say in Kyoto, "Oishii!" or delicious!

Basic Tofu Marinade

I like to use this marinade as a base flavor for grilling, baking, and stir-fry dishes. Keep some on hand and use it to steam with some good organic veggies. Then drizzle on a dressing or sauce, and serve with a grain and maybe some cooked beans and Gomasio (page 95).

Kids enjoy the simple steamed dish. You can entertain them by cutting the tofu into cute shapes with a cookie cutter instead of just slicing.

14–16 oz firm Chinese-style tofu, drained
 ⅓ cup soy sauce
 ⅓ cup rice vinegar
 ⅓ cup water
 1 tsp freshly grated ginger

....

Slice tofu into 6 or 8 slices. Place in a baking dish, trying not to overlap.

In a bowl, mix together the soy sauce, rice vinegar, water, and ginger. Pour marinade over tofu slices. Let marinate 20–30 minutes. You can keep the tofu in the marinade up to 24 hours before it gets too strongly flavored.

VARIATIONS

• *For a lemon version, substitute lemon juice for rice vinegar and 1½ tablespoons sea salt for soy sauce, and omit the ginger. This is good for Le Benedict Florentine (page 224) and when you want a whiter tofu with a bit of a tangy base flavor.*
• *Add 1 clove finely minced garlic.*
• *Add some dried or fresh herbs to create other flavor bases, such as 1 teaspoon curry powder (Indian), ½ teaspoon five-spice powder (Chinese), 2 teaspoons finely chopped fresh lemon grass (Thai), ½ teaspoon dried ground coriander, and ½ teaspoon dried ground cumin (Mexican).*

There is no standard-sized tofu package; they range from 12 to 16 ounces. So if a recipe calls for 1 pound, you may have to use a little less or buy two packages—or use your imagination!

MAKE YOUR OWN

There are some great soy milk machines on the market that include tofu-making kits. They really make the process clean and simple, and you can experience fresh tofu for dinner, it's that quick! Check our web site (www.nativefoods.com) for details.

STORING AND FREEZING TOFU

When storing unused tofu after the package has been opened, make sure it is covered with fresh water and the water is changed daily.

If you want to freeze uncooked tofu, be aware that it will take on a different texture after thawing. To freeze, drain the tofu, then wrap it in plastic wrap or place it in a covered plastic container, and put it in the freezer. Let defrost and pull apart in pieces. Try adding some to soups and stews for a new chewy texture.

part two

The Recipes

complement with condiments

*T*hese recipes can make simple meals simply delicious. Most of them can be made ahead of time and kept in dry storage or refrigerated until you need them. They are a handy way to make food tasty quickly. Simply serve them with grains, beans, and veggies, get ideas from the Serving Suggestions, or make up your own!

Roasted Garlic Cloves

1 CUP

Roasting garlic, as with any root, brings out the stored sugars, so it's not as biting as raw garlic. This is the kind you can kiss with—it actually makes your kisses sweeter!

1 cup peeled garlic cloves
½ cup olive oil
1 tsp salt
¼ tsp black pepper
⅛ tsp crushed red chilies

• •

Preheat oven to 425°F. Place ingredients in a small baking dish such as a loaf pan (10 x 5 x 3 inches). Bake for 20–25 minutes, until golden brown. Serve warm, or let cool before putting in a jar to refrigerate. This will keep up to 3 weeks in the refrigerator.

SERVING SUGGESTIONS

• *Garlic cloves can be used to adorn a pasta dish or pizza, mashed on top of French bread or toast for Garlic Toast (see page 87), or mixed into Italian Salsa (page 120) for extra pizzazz.*
• *After cooling, purée the entire batch in a blender, and use it as a spread for bread at the dinner table or as a flavor enhancer for soups, sauces, and salad dressings.*
• Roasted Garlic Oil: *Pour off the excess oil and save this garlic-infused oil for general cooking or salad dressings.*

Garlic Toast

4–6 SERVINGS

6 slices French bread or sourdough or your favorite

10 Roasted Garlic Cloves (page 86)

2–3 Tbsp Roasted Garlic Oil (see "Serving Suggestions" in Roasted Garlic Cloves recipe)

½ tsp paprika, optional

Mash ingredients together in a mortar and pestle, or in a small bowl with a fork, and spread on bread slices. Toast in a toaster oven or place under the broiler until browned.

Toasted Almond and Currant Chutney

1 CUP

1 cup orange juice

½ cup chopped onion

½ cup currants

1 garlic clove, finely chopped

1 tsp grated fresh ginger

1 Tbsp maple syrup

1 tsp paprika

½ tsp turmeric

½ tsp sea salt

⅓ tsp cayenne

¼ cup apple cider vinegar

¼ cup chopped or sliced almonds, roasted

....

Mix all ingredients except nuts in a stainless steel saucepan and bring to a boil; then let simmer on low heat for 15 minutes, stirring occasionally. Remove from stove and stir in almonds. Store in refrigerator.

Cucumber Quick Pickles

APPROX. 1 ½ CUPS

1 large cucumber or 2 Japanese cucumbers

½ cup soy sauce

½ cup water

If using the large cucumber, peel, slice in half lengthwise, remove seeds with a teaspoon, and cut in ⅓ inch slices on a diagonal. If using a Japanese cucumber, there's no need to take out the seeds; just cut into ⅓-inch slices on a diagonal. Place cucumber slices in a serving bowl.

Combine soy sauce and water, and pour over the cucumbers. Let sit 5 minutes. You can reuse the soy sauce–water mixture for the next one or two batches of cucumber pickles. Store it in the refrigerator in the interim.

SERVING SUGGESTION

Sprinkle with Toasted Sesame Seeds (page 94) and a splash of rice vinegar, and use as a side salad.

Pretty Pink Pickles

2 CUPS

2 cups sliced daikon radish

2 Tbsp umeboshi paste

1½ cups water

....

Bring water and umeboshi paste to a boil in a saucepan. Add daikon slices and let simmer 10 minutes. Cool before serving, and store in refrigerator.

SERVING SUGGESTION

Serve as an accompaniment for sandwiches or cooked grain and veggies with sauce of choice.

Curried Cashew Crunch

1½ CUPS

It's satisfying to have something crunchy to toss on top of salads or warm dishes once in a while. You can even put out for munchies at cocktail or elixir hour.

1 cup raw cashews

½ tsp turmeric

¼ tsp ground cumin

¼ tsp whole fennel seeds

¼ tsp ground coriander

1 Tbsp toasted sesame oil

2 Tbsp soy sauce

½ cup currants

Heat cashews in a dry skillet over medium-high heat, stirring until browned, approximately 2 minutes. Turn to medium-low heat and add toasted sesame oil to skillet, then the dried spices, and toss for 30 seconds. Add soy sauce and stir to coat nuts. Remove from heat and toss in currants. Cool before serving.

Country Croutons

Keep on hand for soups, salads, and casseroles.

8 slices day-old bread, cut into ½-inch cubes

¼ cup olive oil

2 garlic cloves, minced

¼ tsp sea salt

2 Tbsp finely chopped fresh parsley

· ·

Preheat oven to 300°F. Put all ingredients in a bowl and toss well. Spread evenly on an ungreased baking sheet and bake 15 minutes. Turn croutons with a spatula and bake another 10 minutes, until all are nicely browned.

VARIATIONS

• *Cut the bread into any shape you desire other than cubes. You can use small cookie cutters of various shapes, such as sunbursts. These are pretty to float on top of a soup serving.*
• *For flavor variety, add other fresh or dried herbs or spices, such as oregano, basil, paprika, or cumin.*

Cranberry Orange Relish

The pearl onions (also known as boiling onions) used in this recipe add a fun touch and give the relish a unique and appetizing look. It is lovely served during the winter holidays and beats out canned cranberry sauce ten to one.

TIP

This gets better the next day, so make it a day early and refrigerate until ready to serve.

VARIATION

Substitute tangerine for orange . . . yum.

SERVING SUGGESTION

Serve with any savory veggie-meat preparation.

1 qt apple juice

1 apple, diced

2 cups pearl onions, fresh or frozen

1 cup currants or raisins

two 3 inch–long cinnamon sticks

2 cups fresh cranberries, rinsed and damaged ones removed

1 orange, zest and juice

zest of 1 lemon

¼ cup maple syrup (more if you prefer a sweeter taste)

1 tsp sea salt

¼ tsp white pepper

....

If using fresh pearl onions, you need to peel them first by filling a saucepan three-quarters full with water and bringing to a boil. Trim the root off each onion and then cut an X lightly with a paring knife at the same end. Drop the onions in the boiling water for 2 minutes; remove and place under running cold water to stop the cooking. Squeeze the uncut end, and out slips the onion (that's the fun part!).

In a saucepan, place the apple juice, diced apple, onions, currants, and cinnamon sticks. Bring to a boil, then lower heat and let simmer for 20 minutes. Add the rest of the ingredients and let simmer another 3–4 minutes.

Toasted Sesame Seeds

The key here is freshly toasting the seeds, rather than buying them already toasted. They are best used right out of the pan or within a week of toasting. As they say, "Ain't nothin' like it!"

TIP

The pan stays hot once you remove it from the stove, and the seeds continue cooking, so remove the toasted seeds from the pan and cool them on a flat dish.

VARIATION

A mixture of half white and black is a pretty and harmonious combination.

1 cup sesame seeds, black or white

. . . .

Rinse seeds well in a strainer. Let them dry in the strainer and then place in a skillet on medium heat. Shake the pan or stir while toasting for about 1–2 minutes, so as not to burn. A slight popping sound will occur, and the aroma will be enticing. Be careful not to burn; it's best to practice once with the white sesame seeds, as the color change is hard to notice on the black ones.

NUTRITIONAL CONTENT

Sesame seeds are high in lecithin, a lipid that is a constituent of every cell in the body; the sheath around the brain, for example, contains lecithin. Sesame seeds also contain vitamins E, B, and F (fatty acids), plus calcium, iron, magnesium, and trace minerals such as silicon, copper, and chrome. They also contain fifteen amino acids.

Gomasio (Sesame Salt)

This Japanese seasoning is the best condiment in the world! Use it instead of table salt.

1 cup Toasted Sesame Seeds (page 94)
2 tsp sea salt

....

Toast the sea salt in the same way you do the sesame seeds, in a dry skillet for a couple of minutes. Grind the sesame seeds and toasted sea salt together in a suribachi or mortar and pestle. Store in a tightly closed jar in the pantry.

SERVING SUGGESTIONS

• *Sprinkle on plain steamed veggies, grains, salads, or soups.*
• *Get everyone else you know to serve it by buying small, cute airtight containers and filling them up to give as gifts!*

THE WONDER OF GOMASIO

Macrobiotics teaches that gomasio, when used daily, is a natural remedy that strengthens our organism and prevents diseases. It is believed to improve the quality of the blood (making it less acidic), strengthen the nervous and immune systems, improve digestion, alleviate irregular menstruation, aid in the production of breast milk, and relieve eye problems. Wow . . .

Miso Lemon Carrottops

Don't throw out the green tops of carrots! Make sure to buy your carrots with the tops and save them for this tasty condiment. They are a nice source of vitamin C.

1 tsp miso

1 tsp toasted sesame oil

1 tsp lemon or orange zest

1 Tbsp water

½ cup water

2 cups carrottops, finely chopped

1 Tbsp Toasted Sesame Seeds (page 94)

In a small mixing bowl, combine miso with toasted sesame oil, lemon or orange zest, and 1 tablespoon water. In a saucepan, bring ½ cup water to a boil and add carrottops. Add miso mixture to center of greens. Cover and cook over low heat for about 7 minutes. Garnish with Toasted Sesame Seeds, and serve warm or chilled.

SERVING SUGGESTIONS

Serve as a vegetable side dish.

Native Ch'is (Nondairy Cheese)

Our alternative to dairy cheese has a rich and creamy texture. I like it best as an addition to a sandwich or taco rather than just by itself.

VARIATIONS

• *If you want to omit the agar flakes, just add the water to the ground cashews and the rest of the ingredients. You will have more of a spread, which can be put into pastry bags and piped out, or spooned onto sandwiches or tacos, or used as a sauce-style topping for steamed veggies.*

• *Place a piece in the freezer until solid, then grate it on the large-hole section of a cheese grater and sprinkle on pizzas or other dishes just at the end cooking, as the Native Ch'i's will warm quickly.*

3 cups water

¾ cup agar flakes (or a 1-oz package)

2 cups raw cashews (unroasted and unsalted)

½ cup lemon juice

2 Tbsp tahini

2 tsp salt

½ tsp garlic powder

½ tsp onion powder

Place agar and water in a saucepan and bring to a boil, whisking occasionally. Turn to simmer for 5 minutes and continue to whisk; the mixture will thicken.

Grind cashews in a blender to form a powder; it shouldn't be coarse. You may need to do it in two batches (1 cup at a time) so that it grinds well. Put all the ground cashews back in the blender and add the lemon juice, tahini, salt, and garlic and onion powders. Then pour in the water-agar mixture. Blend until smooth and creamy.

Pour into an oiled loaf pan and refrigerate until firm. Slice and serve. Store in refrigerator.

WHEN SMILING FOR A PHOTO, SAY "CH'IIIII'S . . . "!

Ch'i (Sometimes spelled *qi*) is the Chinese word for both the vital life force in the individual and the primordial cosmic energy of the universe. In traditional Chinese medicine, good food is among the important sources of health-giving *ch'i*. And macrobiotics emphasizes that fresh, whole foods keep our *ch'i* in balance, whereas refined, processed foods are deficient in *ch'i*.

Tofu Ricotta

1 lb medium or firm Chinese-style tofu, drained

¼ cup basil chiffonade

¼ cup chopped fresh parsley

¼ cup chopped green onions

3 garlic cloves, minced

2 tsp tahini

1 tsp sea salt

¼ tsp black pepper

Crumble tofu in bowl, add rest of ingredients, and mix and mash until mixture resembles the texture of ricotta.

SERVING SUGGESTIONS

• *Use as a spread for sandwiches, or appetizer canapés with a little Italian Salsa (page 120).*

• *This is the filling for the Eggplant Rollatini (page 229).*

Tofu Feta

Finally a feta that's fit for
PETA (People for the Ethical
Treatment of Animals).

1 lb firm Chinese-style tofu (not silken)

1½ cups Greek Lemon Garlic Dressing (page 106)

½ tsp sea salt

1 tsp dried oregano

....

Cut tofu into ¼-inch cubes or crumble into pieces about
that size. In a mixing bowl, toss tofu with dressing, salt, and
oregano. Let marinate at least 30 minutes. Store in the refrigerator, and use within a week.

SERVING SUGGESTION

Keep on hand and toss in salads or use on pizzas or in wraps.

Salsa de Chupacabra

2 CUPS

This is hot and spicy but full-flavored, and not a burning, bitter heat. It is named after the mysterious "goat-sucker" from South America, a legendary creature, kind of like the Loch Ness Monster, that is said to have come up through Mexico and found its way to California, where it ravaged farm animals without mercy. Since no one has ever seen one, I decided to create a recipe version, which is of course sympathetic to farm animals but beasty to the tastebuds.

1 lb tomatillos
4 Anaheim chilies (long green mild ones)
½ canned chipotle chili
½ cup rice vinegar
½ cup water
2 tsp salt

Preheat oven to broil (500°F). Remove the outer husks from the tomatillos, and arrange the tomatillos with the Anaheim chilies on a baking tray. Broil until the skins are blistered on all sides. Place Anaheim chilies in a bowl covered with plastic or in a plastic bag. Let cool, then remove the outer skins and seeds. Put all ingredients in a blender and purée. When you open the blender lid, stand back a bit, as the fumes can be potent. Pour salsa in a container and store in refrigerator, for up to 3 weeks.

TIP

This dish has high heat decibels, owing to the chilies, so make sure you wash your hands after handling it, and don't touch your eyes after touching the chilies or getting the salsa on your hands.

Ray's Good Home Blackening Spice

ABOUT 1¼ CUPS

Blackening spice is a blend that lends itself to Cajun-style dishes. It is rubbed on food, which is then seared by placing it in a very hot cast-iron skillet to "blacken" (see page 44), creating a dark, spicy crust.

My business partner, Ray, was known for his preparation of blackened seafood and prime rib dishes in the restaurants he owned back in the days before he was a card-carrying vegetarian. Now he's an expert at blackening tempeh and "save the chicken"!

¼ cup cayenne

¼ cup paprika

¼ cup chili powder

2 Tbsp dried oregano

2 Tbsp sea salt

2 Tbsp dried thyme

½ tsp black pepper

¼ tsp ground allspice

¼ tsp garlic powder

¼ tsp ground mace

....

In a small mixing bowl, combine all the spices well. Store in a tightly sealed jar to keep fresh, and store in the refrigerator to keep fresher longer.

Caramelized Onions

ABOUT 1½ CUPS

It is the slow sautéing that brings out the sweetness of the natural sugars stored in the bulb.

3 large onions, cut into thin half-moon slices

3 Tbsp olive or sunflower oil

1 tsp sea salt

¼ tsp white pepper

1 tsp maple syrup (optional)

Heat the olive oil in a skillet, add the onions with a pinch of the salt, and sauté until slightly transparent. Add salt and white pepper, and reduce heat to low. Continue stirring while cooking the onions, uncovered, for about 40–45 minutes. They will appear very brown but not burned. Just before removing them from the heat, stir in maple syrup for an extra special glaze of flavor.

get dressed!

I'm always so amazed when I go into the supermarket and see a full wall of salad dressings, yet there is not a single one that I can use because they contain nonvegan ingredients such as dairy products, or additives like high-fructose corn sweetener and stabilizers. When traveling in Italy, I always loved stopping at the delis for takeout, where they'd have little packets of dressing to go with your salads; the ingredients were olive oil, vinegar, salt, and pepper. What a concept!

All the dressings in this chapter are tasty on fresh organic salads. Get in the habit of keeping a bowl of salad ingredients in the refrigerator, and keep a couple of dressings on hand all the time. When you get in the mood for a snack, train yourself (and the kids, please!) to make a salad and enjoy it with a homemade dressing. Add toasted nuts, a cooked grain, some cooked beans. . . . See how easy it is to eat well and quickly? Best of all, it's not boring, as the foods you see every day at the markets or restaurants can become!

Basic Balsamic Vinaigrette

We get a lot of requests at the restaurant regarding how to make this dressing. It's simple, has a very satisfying flavor, and is easy to make.

½ cup chopped onion

½ cup balsamic vinegar

½ cup olive oil

1½ tsp sea salt

½ tsp black pepper

Purée onion and vinegar in a blender. With blender on low speed, gradually add oil, salt, and pepper.

TIP

If your blender doesn't have a low speed for adding oils slowly, pour the vinegar mixture into a bowl and slowly whisk in the oil, salt, and pepper.

VARIATIONS

• *Add different fresh herbs, such as marjoram or oregano.*
• *Add 1 teaspoon Dijon mustard and decrease the salt to 1 teaspoon.*
• *Substitute chopped shallots for the onion.*
• *Substitute other types of vinegar such as white wine, champagne, or raspberry.*

Green Goddess

2½ CUPS

1 shallot, peeled and chopped

½ cup fresh parsley leaves, loosely packed

½ cup chopped green onions

½ cup white wine vinegar or tarragon vinegar

1½ cups olive oil

1½ tsp salt

¼ tsp black pepper

· ·

Purée shallot, parsley, green onions, and vinegar in a blender. With blender on low speed, gradually add oil, salt, and pepper.

THE ORIGIN OF GREEN GODDESS

When George Arliss, the famous 1920s actor, was opening in San Francisco in *The Green Goddess,* a play by William Archer, the Palace Hotel chef, Philip Roemer, created a version of this dressing in his honor. I did a little research on George Arliss and found a lovely quote from him: "Humility is the only true wisdom by which we prepare our minds for all the possible changes of life." Furthermore, I found out he was very health-minded and actually had quite a bit to say about the effects of eating meat and disease. You can see why I had to include this recipe in the book!

Greek Lemon Garlic Dressing

I ½ CUPS

1 cup olive oil

½ cup lemon juice (juice from about 2 lemons)

2 garlic cloves, minced

½ tsp salt

¼ tsp black pepper

Put all ingredients in a jar, blender, or bowl, and shake, purée, or whisk.

Mango Lime Vinaigrette

I CUP

This dressing is thick, so you may need to drizzle it on salads using a spoon.

1 cup chopped fresh or frozen mango
½ cup safflower or sunflower oil
¼ cup maple syrup
¼ cup lime juice
1 Tbsp rice vinegar
1½ tsp sea salt
1½ tsp grated fresh ginger

Place all ingredients in a blender and purée. When I use frozen mango, I sometimes put it in frozen, since blending defrosts it. Alternatively you may defrost the mango first.

VARIATION

Substitute tangerine juice for lime juice, and call it Mango Tango Vinaigrette.

SERVING SUGGESTION

Check out the Mecca Azteca Salad (page 167), which uses this dressing, and see why it's one of our most requested specials.

Pumpkin Plum Dressing

1 ½ CUPS

1¼ cups water

1 cup raw pumpkin seeds

2 tsp umeboshi plum paste

....

Purée all ingredients in a blender until creamy.

Ponzu (Japanese Soy Citrus Dressing)

1 ½ CUPS

This is a great dipping sauce
as well as a superb dressing
for salad greens and grains.
Some versions of ponzu
contain fish stock, but not
this one!

½ cup soy sauce

¼ cup rice vinegar

¼ cup lemon juice

½ cup water

2 Tbsp toasted sesame oil

....

Put all ingredients in a jar and shake well.

VARIATION

Add 1 teaspoon grated ginger or 1 teaspoon grated daikon radish.

Sesame Orange Vinaigrette

2 CUPS

This dressing is what makes our Chinese "Save the Chicken" Salad (page 179) so famous among our customers. It's a good dressing for Thai Slaw (page 188) as well.

½ cup orange juice

¼ cup rice vinegar

¼ cup maple syrup

2 Tbsp grated ginger

1 Tbsp finely minced lemon grass (optional)

¾ cup safflower or sunflower oil

¼ cup toasted sesame oil

1 Tbsp sea salt

¼ tsp white pepper

• •

Purée orange juice, rice vinegar, maple syrup, ginger, and lemon grass in a blender. With blender on low speed, gradually add oils, salt, and white pepper.

Thousand Island Dressing

1 ¼ CUPS

This dressing adds a pleasantly familiar touch to salads or sandwiches. I like to use it instead of mayo in spicier sandwiches.

1 cup vegan mayonnaise

2 Tbsp minced onion

1 Tbsp sweet pickle relish

¼ cup catsup

Mix all ingredients together in a bowl.

Caesar's Vegan

2 CUPS

1 cup olive oil

¾ cup water

¼ cup miso

¼ cup lemon juice

2 garlic cloves, chopped

1 Tbsp capers

¾ tsp sea salt

¼ tsp black pepper

⅛ tsp white pepper

· ·

Purée all ingredients in a blender.

SERVING SUGGESTION

This is great for the California Caesar (page 169) and is one of my favorite quick toppings for simple steamed or blanched leafy greens.

Black Creek Ranch Dressing

2 CUPS

Black Creek Ranch in San Antonio, Texas, was a hunting ranch and cattle-raising facility for years, until one great woman turned it into a 1,200-acre sanctuary. I was privileged to cook there and pet the cows. This dressing is named after that soon-to-be-famous compassionate ranch.

1$\frac{1}{4}$ cup vegan mayonnaise

$\frac{1}{4}$ tsp garlic powder

$\frac{1}{4}$ tsp onion powder

$\frac{1}{4}$ tsp sea salt

$\frac{1}{2}$ tsp black pepper

2 tsp finely chopped parsley

$\frac{3}{4}$ cup soy milk

....

Whisk all ingredients together in a bowl.

Curry Lime Vinaigrette

2 CUPS

2 Tbsp toasted sesame oil

3 Tbsp curry powder

½ cup coconut milk

½ cup safflower or sunflower oil

1 garlic clove, chopped

1 tsp minced ginger

⅓ cup maple syrup or organic sugar

½ cup chopped cilantro

½ cup soy sauce

¼ cup lime juice

· ·

Heat toasted sesame oil in small skillet. When the oil is hot (but not to the point of smoking), add curry powder and stir for about 5 seconds, being careful not to burn it. This brings out the curry flavor. Blend all ingredients, including the sesame oil–curry mixture, in a blender.

SERVING SUGGESTION

I love this dressing tossed with salad greens, quinoa, chopped sautéed tempeh, and a few raisins.

Madison's Garden Dressing

1 ½ CUPS

This dressing is too hip to be square, just like Deborah Madison's garden! Use it on all your salads and vegetables, and even as a light sauce or glaze on cooked meat alternatives.

1 cup pitted fresh or frozen cherries
¼ cup olive oil
¼ cup balsamic vinegar
¼ cup water
¼ cup roasted pistachios
2 Tbsp chopped red onion
1 Tbsp chopped fresh mint
1 tsp maple syrup
½ tsp sea salt
⅛ tsp black pepper
2 Tbsp coarsely chopped pistachios

Put all ingredients in a blender except the 2 tablespoons coarsely chopped pistachios, and purée. Pour into a container and stir in the chopped pistachios, which gives a little texture and more pistachio flavor bites.

SERVING SUGGESTIONS

• *Drizzle on Summer Grilled Vegetables (page 270) or use as a dip for a veggie crudités platter.*
• *For a refreshing dessert, use atop some fresh fruit with soy vanilla ice cream or summer melons.*

get sauced!

I suggest always having at least two of the sauces prepared and in the refrigerator, waiting for you to come home to use for a quick and hearty meal.

Gandhi's Curry Sauce

2 CUPS

One day I was pondering
Mahatma Gandhi's life and
decided to prepare an Indian
dish for supper, and when I
made the sauce I named it
for him. If you read his autobiography (*An Autobiography:
The Story of My Experiments
with Truth*), you'll know why
I was inspired by this compassionate vegetarian man,
and you'll probably think the
sauce tastes even better!

1½ cups canned coconut milk
1 cup fresh cilantro leaves, loosely packed
½ cup water
¼ cup safflower or sunflower oil
¼ cup soy sauce
¼ cup maple syrup
2 garlic cloves, chopped
2 Tbsp curry powder
2 tsp grated fresh ginger
½ tsp crushed red chili (optional)

Place all ingredients in a blender and purée.

TIP

*The spiciness of commercial curry powders varies, so you may
want to measure to taste and use less if you don't like it too
hot. However, in my experience, most varieties sold at groceries and natural foods markets are very mild.*

SERVING SUGGESTION

Accompanies the Gandhi Bowl (page 214).

Simple Marinara

3 CUPS

The fewer ingredients you use, the better it will be. Experiment with the different flavors of fresh herbs by adding them when you take sauce off the stovetop.

¼ cup olive oil

½ cup finely chopped onion

3 garlic cloves, sliced

28 oz can chopped or crushed peeled tomatoes

½ tsp sea salt

¼ tsp black pepper

½ cup fresh basil chiffonade (page 45)

Heat olive oil in a saucepan, and sauté onion and garlic until transparent and lightly browned. Add tomatoes, salt, and pepper, and let simmer 10–15 minutes. Remove from heat and add basil just before serving. If making sauce ahead of time, add basil after rewarming, before serving.

Baja Enchilada

Follow directions for Simple Marinara (page 118) and add 1 teaspoon ground coriander and 1 teaspoon ground cumin to onion and garlic when sautéeing. Then, instead of basil, substitute ½ teaspoon chipotle chili powder or ½ teaspoon juice from canned chipotle chilies.

Italian Salsa

2 CUPS

2 cups chopped fresh tomato

2 garlic cloves, minced

½ cup basil chiffonade (see page 45)

1 Tbsp olive oil

½ tsp sea salt

¼ tsp black pepper

....

Mix all ingredients in a bowl.

VARIATION

Toss in 2–3 tablespoons whole Roasted Garlic Cloves (page 86).

Salsa Fresca

2 CUPS

Start with this recipe, add
some guacamole, some tor-
tilla chips, some Neato Refritos (page 269), and some
Tijuana Tacos (page 205),
and let the fiesta begin!

2 cups chopped fresh tomatoes
½ cup chopped red onion
1 cup lightly chopped fresh cilantro
¼ cup lime juice
1½ tsp sea salt

....

Mix all ingredients in a bowl.

VARIATION

Add chopped avocado and fresh corn kernels.

Thai Peanut Sauce

2 ½ CUPS

This sauce is Native-famous with Thai Sticks (page 150).

2–3 Tbsp safflower or sunflower oil

1 cup chopped onion

4 garlic cloves, sliced

1½ cups canned coconut milk

¾ cup whole unsalted peanuts, roasted (see page 46)

¾ cup rice vinegar

¼ cup maple syrup

¼ cup soy sauce

½ tsp crushed red chili flakes (optional)

Heat oil in a skillet, and sauté onion and garlic until transparent and lightly browned. Place garlic and onion mixture in a blender with all other ingredients, and blend until smooth.

Pumpkin Seed Pesto

I CUP

This is a concentrated flavor base, so you'll only need to use a bit at a time.

It's a great way to use fresh basil when you get a lot of it, whether in the garden or the farmers' market when it's so big and beautiful you can't resist buying huge bunches.

1 cup basil leaves, lightly packed

¾ cup olive oil

½ cup pumpkin seeds, raw or toasted

2 garlic cloves, chopped

1 Tbsp sea salt

1 tsp lemon juice

Purée all ingredients in a blender. The pesto will keep in a tightly covered jar in the refrigerator for up to 3 weeks.

VARIATIONS

- *Substitute pine nuts for pumpkin seeds.*
- *Substitute ¼ cup fresh rosemary for the 1 cup of basil leaves.*

Creamy Wild Mushroom

2 ½ CUPS

Check out the exotic mushroom section at the market
and have fun choosing things
you've never used before.
Mix and match!

TIP

*If you want to try a packet of
dried porcini mushrooms in
the blend, you'll need to reconstitute them first. Use the
soak water in the sauce for
extra flavor, but avoid the
sand and gritty particles at
the bottom of the bowl used
for soaking.*

SERVING SUGGESTION

*Lovely with sautéed tempeh or
seitan.*

3 Tbsp olive oil

4 shallots, thinly sliced

4 oz mushrooms (your choice), sliced
   pinch sea salt

2 Tbsp unbleached flour

2 cups soy milk

½ cup white wine

½ tsp sea salt

¼ tsp white pepper

....

In a saucepan, sauté shallots in olive oil until translucent
and lightly browned. Add mushrooms and a pinch of the
salt. Sauté 1 minute, then sprinkle on the flour, and stir
until it is absorbed. Slowly stir in soy milk, white wine, salt,
and white pepper. Simmer until slightly thickened.

Shallot Mushroom Gravy

2 CUPS

If you are not fond of mushrooms, just omit them and call it Classic Brown Gravy.

3 Tbsp olive oil

5 peeled shallots, finely chopped

1 lb button mushrooms, sliced

2 cups Simple Deglaze (page 65)

3 Tbsp kuzu, dissolved in ⅓ cup water

....

In a saucepan, sauté shallots in olive oil until lightly browned. Add mushrooms and sauté 2–3 minutes. Add Deglaze and let simmer 2 more minutes. Add kuzu dissolved in water, and stir until slightly thickened. Remove from heat.

VARIATION
Add ¼ cup white wine when adding the Deglaze.

SERVING SUGGESTIONS
- *Try it with the Tempeh Scaloppine (page 215).*
- *Great with Roasted Garlic Mashed Potatoes (page 218).*
- *Try it over some sautéed seitan.*

Sassy Sweet and Sour Sauce

3 CUPS

1 Tbsp miso

1 cup Simple Deglaze (page 65)

1½ cups apple juice

½ cup maple syrup

2 Tbsp grated fresh ginger

1 Tbsp whole-grain mustard

½ cup rice vinegar

3 Tbsp kuzu, dissolved in ½ cup water

juice and zest of 1 orange

....

Dissolve the miso in a small amount of Deglaze. In a saucepan, combine all the ingredients except the kuzu-water mixture and the orange zest and juice. Heat over medium-high heat until almost boiling. Add kuzu mixture and orange zest and juice. Stir until mixture thickens and is almost boiling. Remove from heat.

SERVING SUGGESTIONS

* Serve with Sweet and Sour Nuggets (page 237).
* Serve over a bowl filled with rice and steamed veggies and maybe some blackened tempeh (see page 44).

Green Tea Sesame Sauce

2 CUPS

½ cup tahini

1 garlic clove, sliced

1 Tbsp grated fresh ginger

¼ cup soy sauce

¼ cup maple syrup

3 Tbsp rice vinegar

1 cup brewed green tea (can substitute bancha or roasted barley tea)

1 tsp toasted sesame oil

Place all ingredients in a blender and blend thoroughly. Warm on stovetop and serve.

SERVING SUGGESTION

Try this sauce on hot udon noodles with steamed marinated tofu (see Basic Tofu Marinade, page 80), vegetables, and sesame seeds.

Bessie's (Thank-You) BBQ Sauce

4 CUPS

¼ cup safflower or sunflower oil

½ cup chopped onion

4 cloves garlic cloves minced

2 tsp chili powder

2 cups tomato purée

1½ cups water

¼ cup maple syrup

¼ cup molasses

¼ cup apple cider vinegar

¼ cup lemon juice

1 Tbsp Dijon mustard

1 Tbsp grated fresh ginger

1½ tsp salt

½ tsp black pepper

. . . .

Sauté onion and garlic in oil in saucepan until transparent and lightly browned. Add chili powder and sauté another minute. Add remaining ingredients and simmer, partially covered, for 30 minutes.

Tartar Sauce

1 ½ CUPS

1 cup vegan mayonnaise

¼ cup finely chopped onion or shallots

2 Tbsp capers

2 Tbsp lemon juice

....

Mix all ingredients together in a bowl.

Jamaican Jerk Marinade

2½ CUPS

2 cups chopped green onion

1 cup apple cider vinegar

1 cup soy sauce

¼ cup safflower or sunflower oil

3 garlic cloves sliced

1 jalapeño pepper with seeds, chopped

1½ tsp allspice

1 tsp nutmeg

1 tsp cinnamon

....

Put all ingredients in a blender and purée.

Flamed Banana Salsa

2 cups Salsa Fresca (page 121)

½ cup Jamaican Jerk Marinade (page 130)

1 banana, peeled and sliced

....

In a skillet, heat Salsa Fresca for about 2 minutes, until hot. Add Jamaican Jerk Marinade and stir for another minute. Lastly, add bananas and toss until they get warmed through.

Rockin' Moroccan Marinade

2 ½ CUPS

1 cup olive oil

1 cup orange juice

¼ cup lemon juice

¼ cup maple syrup

3 garlic cloves, sliced

2 Tbsp paprika

1 Tbsp grated fresh ginger

1 Tbsp oregano

1 Tbsp turmeric

2 tsp thyme

½ tsp cinnamon

1 tsp cayenne

1 tsp salt

....

Purée all ingredients in a blender. Rock it or lose it!

SERVING SUGGESTIONS

Use with Steak Morocco (page 232) or as a marinade for tofu and vegetables.

Hollandaise Sauce

1 CUP

1 Tbsp olive oil

1 shallot, finely chopped

1 cup soy milk

1½ Tbsp fresh lemon juice

1½ tsp dried tarragon

½ tsp sea salt

⅛ tsp turmeric

pinch white pepper

pinch cayenne pepper

1½ Tbsp kuzu, dissolved in ¼ cup water

· ·

Heat oil in a saucepan and sauté shallots until translucent and lightly browned. Put mixture in a blender with ½ cup of the soy milk and blend well. Pour back into pot and whisk in other ingredients except the kuzu. Add kuzu-water mixture and stir until thickened.

SERVING SUGGESTION

Perfect for Le Benedict Florentine (page 224) for breakfast or brunch.

snacks 'n' apps

*T*hese are some recipes that have been favorites of both my restaurant customers and cooking-class students. They may get you the "host with the most" award or just through the day!

Edamame (Sweet Green Soybeans)

TIP

Frozen edamame can be pur-chased already shelled—not as much fun to eat but great for using in soups or as garnishes on salads and entrées for their pretty green color.

NUTRITIONAL CONTENT

One-half cup cooked edamame has 8 grams protein and 35 mg isoflavones (the recommended serving is 25–40 mg per day).

I always use the mnemonic "and yo' mama" to remember the pronunciation of these sweet beans: ed-ah-MAH-meh. These are the green soybeans in their pods before they are dried. They are easily found in the frozen section at many markets, including supermarkets now. Try to make sure you buy non-GMO (genetically modified organisms) and preferably organic! They can be found fresh in late summer at farmers' markets or Asian markets where bunches of the whole bush are sold. The bush is about two feet in height; the pod is cute and fuzzy and usually has two or three beans per pod.

Edamame are delightful steamed and eaten warm, dusted with sea salt. In warmer weather they can be cooked and then chilled for a refreshing snack.

The way to eat them is to insert the whole pod in your mouth while holding the other end. Slowly pull the pod out of your mouth, thereby lightly scraping off the soft, lightly salted flesh of the outer portion of the pod with your teeth while removing the beans from the inside. Kids love them, and they are oh so nutritious.

3 cups water
8 oz (approx. ½ bag) frozen edamame
½ tsp sea salt

· ·

Bring water to boil in a saucepan, add edamame, and cook for 3–4 minutes. Drain in a colander and toss with sea salt.

Harry's Hummus

1 ½ CUPS

This recipe is a Greek-style hummus, which doesn't include tahini. This gives it a lighter essence.

1 cup cooked garbanzo beans
¼ cup garbanzo cooking liquid
2 garlic cloves, peeled and sliced
⅓ cup extra-virgin olive oil
¼ cup lemon juice
½ tsp sea salt

....

Purée all ingredients in a blender until smooth. It may be necessary to add more cooking liquid or water to create a smooth texture.

VARIATION

Add 2 tablespoons raw or roasted tahini.

Ruth's Awesome Threesome

6 SERVINGS
(OR 2 THREESOMES)

This was inspired by my dear
friend Ruth's good taste.

2 cups Italian Salsa (page 120)

12 or more Roasted Garlic Cloves (page 86)

1 cup Harry's Hummus (page 136)

6 slices olive bread, toasted and brushed with
Roasted Garlic Oil (page 86)

1 large fresh basil leaf

1 slice fresh lemon

....

Mix Italian Salsa with Roasted Garlic Cloves and place in a
small serving bowl. Place hummus in a small serving bowl.
Garnish salsa bowl with a large pretty basil leaf, and garnish
hummus with freshly chopped parsley and a lemon slice.
Cut toasted olive bread in thirds and serve with Italian
Salsa and hummus. Invite guests to spread some of each on
the bread.

SERVING SUGGESTION

*Serve with a good crusty French or dark bread, pita toasts, or
lavosh crisps.*

VARIATION

*Make it a foursome and serve with Tata's Tapenade (page 140)
or Papa's Yugoslavian Ivar (page 144).*

Tempeh Pâté

APPROX. 1 ½ CUPS

This is soul-satisfying. Use
with leftover sautéed tempeh
patties, if you ever have any.

4 tempeh patties prepared according to
   Tempeh Basic Prep (page 65)
¼ cup vegan mayonnaise
½ cup chopped green onions
½ cup chopped fresh dill
¼ tsp sea salt

....

Chop tempeh patties into small ½-inch cubes or crumble
by hand and place in bowl. Add the rest of ingredients and
mix well.

VARIATIONS

• *Put this on bagels or in sandwiches or wraps (see Palm
Springs Wrap, page 196).*
• *If you don't mash the tempeh too much when mixing and
leave it a little chunky, it is more like a "country-style" pâté.*
• *Try blending it in a food processor, you may have to add a
little more vegan mayonnaise to blend well; then put in pastry
bag and pipe on small toasts or crackers.*
• *Double the recipe, then form into a ball shape and roll in 1
cup of roasted and ground pecans. Reminiscent of, but much
better than, those old cheese balls. Serve with crackers.*

French Love Bites

1½ cups Tempeh Pâté (page 138)
1 sheet frozen prepared puff pastry

Garnish
½ cup cherry or cranberry jelly
2 Tbsp freshly chopped parsley or chives

Preheat oven to 425°F. Remove one sheet of puff pastry from the freezer and leave it at room temperature about 20 minutes, until slightly softened. Lightly dust a clean, hard surface with a little flour, and lightly roll out the pastry sheet into an 8½ x 11–inch rectangle. Cut puff pastry sheet in half. On each half of puff pastry spoon half of Tempeh Paté along the longer length and roll paté inside.

Place on ungreased cookie sheet and bake 25 minutes, until puffed and golden brown. Remove from oven and let cool for about 10–15 minutes; then cut in rounds or at a slight diagonal to create bite-size portions. Top with a dollop of cherry or cranberry jelly. Garnish with freshly chopped parsley or chives. Serve warm.

Tata's Tapenade

1 CUP

A tapenade is an olive and caper paste originating in southern France. It usually contains lemon juice, olive oil and anchovies. Here the anchovies are omitted but not missed.

VARIATIONS

• *Substitute fresh rosemary or basil for thyme leaves.*
• *Try a mild green olive, like a Graber olive instead of Niçoise, or mix and match!*

1 Tbsp capers, drained
1 tsp grated lemon zest
1 garlic clove
1 cup pitted Niçoise olives
¼ cup extra virgin olive oil
1 tsp lemon juice
½ tsp fresh thyme leaves

Using a mortar and pestle, grind the capers, lemon zest, and garlic into a smooth paste. Add the olives and grind into a coarse paste. Put paste in mixing bowl and stir in the olive oil, lemon juice, and thyme leaves. The tapenade will keep well in the refrigerator for a few weeks.

SERVING SUGGESTIONS

• *Serve on bread or on sandwiches with veggie meats.*
• *Use as a condiment with cooked grains, veggies, or navy or cannelli beans.*
• *Add a dollop to a pasta dish for a Mediterranean swing.*

Spanakopita

20–24 PIECES

VARIATION

*Add Italian Ground Around
(page 75) on top of the spinach
mixture when layering.*

SERVING SUGGESTION

*Serve in larger portions as an
entrée with Gorgeous Greek
Salad (page 181).*

2 bunches fresh spinach, cleaned well and stems
  removed

2–3 Tbsp olive oil

1 onion, finely chopped

1 tsp dried oregano

8 oz firm Chinese-style tofu (not silken), drained

2 tsp lemon juice

1¼ tsp sea salt

¼ tsp black pepper

1 package filo dough

¼ cup olive oil

....

Preheat oven to 400°F. Steam spinach until just wilted;
drain and chop. Chop tofu into ¼-inch squares or crumble
by hand into pieces approximately that size.

In a skillet, sauté onion in the olive oil until transparent
and lightly browned, about 5 minutes. Add chopped
steamed spinach, oregano, tofu, lemon juice, salt, and pepper. Reduce heat and cook another 2 minutes. Mix well to
disperse seasonings. Remove from heat and let slightly cool.

Ready a 13 x 9 x 2–inch baking pan and the ¼ cup oil.
Using a pastry brush, lightly coat the bottom of the baking
pan with oil.

Remove filo dough sheets and unroll. Take out half and
replace the other half in plastic wrap and put back in the

box. Brush each filo sheet lightly and quickly with oil, one sheet at a time, and line the bottom of the pan with 6 sheets. Spoon and spread half of spinach mixture on top of the filo. Repeat the filo layers, using 6 more sheets. Spoon and spread on the rest of spinach mixture. Top with 6 more oiled filo sheets.

Bake for 25 minutes until golden brown. Let cool enough to cut into squares, and serve.

Zen Cucumber Bites

20–30 PIECES

VARIATIONS

• *During the holiday season, substitute pomegranate seeds for chopped red bell pepper.*
• *Use the cucumber–cream cheese base, and instead of the ginger, sesame, dill, and bell pepper, put on a dollop of Italian Salsa (page 120) with a small fresh basil leaf for garnish.*
• *Use Salsa Fresca (page 121), with fresh cilantro and freshly cooked or defrosted frozen corn kernels for garnish.*

2 Japanese cucumbers (or 1 large hothouse cucumber)
8 oz soy cream cheese
½ cup soy milk
1 jar pickled ginger slices
½ cup fresh dill sprigs
2 Tbsp toasted black and white sesame seeds
2–3 Tbsp Brunoise-cut red bell pepper (see page 45)

....

Wash cucumbers and score the outside skin lengthwise with a fork. Cut at a slight angle to achieve about a ¼-inch thickness (so that it can be picked up easily).

Lay cucumber slices on a tray. Put cream cheese in a bowl, and whisk in soy milk to slightly thin cream cheese. Put a small dollop of cream cheese on each cucumber round. Top with a slice of pickled ginger, a pinch of sesame seeds, a dill sprig, and a square or two of the Brunoise-cut red bell pepper. Picture-pretty and ready to serve!

Papa's Yugoslavian Ivar

6–8 SERVINGS

A favorite my mother always kept in the refrigerator for my father. When I got a little older and my friends discovered its flavor, it was harder to keep in supply.

VARIATION

Purée half or all of recipe in a blender for a smoother texture.

SERVING SUGGESTIONS

• *Best served on crusty French, pita toasts, or lavosh crisps.*
• *Add a dollop to a pasta dish for a little extra bang.*

1 yellow bell pepper

2 red bell peppers

1 medium eggplant

1 garlic clove, minced

¼ tsp minced jalapeño

3 Tbsp sunflower or safflower oil

3 Tbsp red wine vinegar

1 tsp salt

¼ tsp black pepper

Roast bell peppers and eggplant on a grill or in the oven broiler until the skins are blistered, turning so that all sides get blistered. When they are well roasted, remove them and place them in bowl and cover with plastic wrap. Let them sit until cool enough to handle, about 15–20 minutes. Remove the skin and seeds from the peppers and the skin from the eggplant, trying not to lose the juice. Save any juice that was in the bowl. Finely chop the eggplant and peppers, and put them in the bowl with the juices. Add rest of ingredients and combine well.

Store in a jar in the refrigerator for up to 3 weeks. The flavors will develop well by the next day after preparation. Serve at room temperature.

Sophie's Stuffed Mushrooms

8–12 SERVINGS

Named after my dog Sophie, who loves them, and food in general—my kinda gal!

VARIATIONS

• *Add ¼ cup currants to the stuffing mix.*
• *Substitute ground or finely chopped hazelnuts or pecans for bread crumbs.*
• *Add ½ teaspoon chopped fresh rosemary in addition to or instead of parsley.*

TIP

Washing mushrooms when preparing tends to wash away their flavor too. I find it best to start with organic mushrooms and wipe them with damp clean cloth or paper towel (make sure to buy recycled paper towels and recycle after using!).

2 dozen medium-sized mushrooms

3 Tbsp olive oil

4 shallots, peeled and minced

½ cup dried bread crumbs

½ cup soy milk

½ tsp sea salt

¼ tsp black pepper

¼ cup chopped parsley

∙∙∙

Preheat oven to 375°F. Carefully remove the stems from the mushroom caps. Wipe mushrooms with a damp cloth or paper towel. Chop mushroom stems fine.

To make stuffing, sauté shallots and chopped mushroom stems in olive oil in a skillet until translucent and lightly browned. Add bread crumbs and sauté another minute. Stir in soy milk, salt, and pepper. Remove from flame and stir in chopped parsley.

Place mushroom caps in a lightly oiled 13 x 9 x 2–inch baking dish. Use a teaspoon to fill the caps with stuffing. Bake for 15 minutes.

Cauliflower Crudité with Sesame Curry Dip

When I thought I was the only one in the world and possibly the universe who wanted to integrate vegetarian cuisine with traditional European and other ethnic flavors, I discovered Annemarie Colbin and her cookbook *The Natural Gourmet*. This is an adaptation of one of her recipes. She recommended using cauliflower, and I agree, as the mellow flavor and light texture go extremely well with the dip. A presentation of cauliflowerets at a party can be spectacular.

½ cup smooth peanut butter

½ cup tahini

¼ cup maple syrup

¼ cup rice vinegar

¼ cup soy sauce

½ cup water

2 tsp toasted sesame oil

2 garlic cloves, minced

1 Tbsp curry powder

¼ tsp cayenne powder

1 medium cauliflower, cut into bite-size florets

....

In a small mixing bowl, combine peanut butter, tahini, maple syrup, rice vinegar, and soy sauce. Add the water gradually to incorporate.

In a small skillet, heat the toasted sesame oil, and add minced garlic, curry powder, and cayenne, and sauté for just a few seconds. Add the oil and spices to the peanut butter and tahini mixture, making sure to scrape the skillet well to remove all the oil and spices. You may add more water if you desire a thinner consistency; also, the dip will become thicker after it sits for a while, so you may want to add more water later as well.

Place the dip in a bowl and put the bowl on a platter. Arrange the cauliflowerets around the bowl. *Now* watch the party get started.

Guacamole

APPROX. 1½ CUPS

2 ripe avocados, peeled and pit removed

2 tsp lime juice

½ tsp sea salt

Place ingredients in a small bowl and mash together. That's it! *¡Muy fácil!*

VARIATIONS

- *Add ½ cup chopped tomato.*
- *Add ½ cup chopped cilantro.*
- *Add ¼ teaspoon chopped jalapeño pepper or canned chipotle pepper juice.*
- *Substitute lemon for lime juice.*

SERVING SUGGESTION

Per tradition, serve with corn tortilla chips and Salsa Fresca (page 121).

Speedy Kim Chee

10—12 SERVINGS

Kim chee is a spicy pickled cabbage from Korea. I was traveling in Korea during the Seoul Olympics and ate lots of kim chee and even visited a kim chee museum. I was also privileged to witness Flo Jo run a race and win a gold medal. This recipe is almost as speedy as I remember her to be, but certainly not as spicy! Awesome inspiration; bless her.

1 medium Napa cabbage

6 cups warm water

2 tsp sea salt

2 green onions, sliced into 1½-inch lengths

5 garlic cloves, minced

1 small red chili, sliced into ⅛-inch rounds

1 Tbsp grated fresh ginger

1½ Tbsp toasted sesame oil

1 Tbsp maple syrup

1 tsp sea salt

½ tsp cayenne powder

Quarter the cabbage lengthwise, leaving the base intact. Fill a large bowl with the warm water and sea salt, and soak the sections of the cabbage until soft, about 5–10 minutes. Drain and rinse with fresh water, cut off base, and set aside.

In a medium-sized bowl, mix together the rest of ingredients. Tear the drained cabbage leaves lengthwise into narrow strips, and toss them with the pepper mixture in the bowl. Wait 5 minutes, then serve.

Native Nachos

4–6 SERVINGS

6 cups corn tortilla chips

1 cup cooked black beans, warmed

1 cup Taco Meat, warmed (page 74)

1 cup Salsa Fresca (page 121)

½ cup Native Ch'i's (Nondairy Cheese, page 97), grated or piped

½ cup Guacamole (page 147)

⅓ cup fresh cilantro leaves

¼ cup chopped green onions

....

Arrange tortilla chips on a large plate or platter. Cover chips with warm black beans and Taco Meat. Then top with Salsa Fresca and Guacamole. Sprinkle grated nondairy cheese, or pipe it with a pastry bag, on and around nacho platter to make a pretty presentation. Garnish with cilantro and green onions.

VARIATIONS

• *Warm tortilla chips before placing on platter.*
• *Add some pickled jalapeño slices as a garnish.*

Thai Sticks

6–8 SERVINGS

2 sautéed tempeh patties (see Tempeh Basic Prep, page 65)

⅓ cup Thai Peanut Sauce (page 122)

⅓ cup fresh cilantro leaves

¼ cup roasted peanuts (unsalted)

1 tsp Brunoise-cut red bell pepper (see page 45)

∙∙

Cut sautéed tempeh patties into 4–5 slices. With a 6- or 8-inch bamboo skewer per tempeh slice, pierce through each end of slice from one end to the other, the long way. Arrange skewers on a plate or platter, and serve the sauce in a little cup on the side. Garnish with cilantro, peanuts, and chopped bell pepper.

VARIATION

Try blackening the tempeh patties (see page 44) for extra flavor power.

soup of the day

Our customers do appreciate a good soup, and while I haven't put the complete top 40 in this chapter, I did include the hit Manilow's Minestrone.

SOUP-MAKING TIPS

• *When making soup, never boil it. When reheating, once it starts to come to a boil, immediately reduce the heat to simmer. It's one of those things that Mom teaches that you don't question. . . . Actually, it's the only thing I didn't question!*

• *When puréeing hot soups in a blender, be careful not to close the lid too securely, as the whole thing could blow up into one big mess and burn you! Let soup cool slightly, then blend in small batches with lid vented. The blenders with a variable speed dial are great because then you can start out very slowly. I always put a kitchen towel over the lid and opening just in case.*

Mighty Miso

4 SERVINGS

A cup of miso a day keeps the doctor away! Try drinking this instead of coffee at breakfast. Get everyone to do it, and then start a chain of soup houses called Buck o' Miso.

Rule number one when preparing miso soup is to never let it boil. This kills the wonderful living culture that makes it so special and healing (see pages 25–26).

2-inch strip wakame

2 dried shitake mushrooms

4 cups water

$\frac{1}{4}$ cup daikon, chopped into $\frac{1}{4}$-inch cubes

1 small carrot, sliced into half moons

$1\frac{1}{2}$ Tbsp miso

$\frac{1}{2}$ cup chopped soft or firm Chinese-style tofu, cut into $\frac{1}{4}$-inch cubes

$\frac{1}{4}$ cup chopped green onion

• •

Soak wakame in warm water to cover for a few minutes. Then rinse with fresh water. Remove the center hard strip (called the stipe), and chop into $\frac{1}{2}$-inch pieces.

Soak shitake mushrooms in warm water to cover for 20 minutes. Remove the hard stem, and slice mushroom caps.

Put 4 cups water in a soup pot with wakame, mushrooms, daikon, and carrot. Bring to a boil, then lower heat and simmer 5–10 minutes.

Put miso in a cup or small bowl with about $\frac{1}{2}$ cup of cooking liquid and mix to dissolve. Add it back to the soup pot with the tofu cubes, and gently simmer 3 minutes. Garnish servings with green onions and enjoy.

Russian Velvet

6–8 SERVINGS

If you could eat velvet, it would probably have a similar texture to this dish. It's a gorgeous red soup that would be great to serve on Valentine's Day.

1 Tbsp olive or sunflower oil

1 large onion, chopped

1 medium carrot, chopped

2 red beets, peeled and chopped

6 cups water

1 cup red lentils, washed and drained

3 bay leaves (optional)

1 Tbsp sea salt

2–3 Tbsp umeboshi vinegar (see page 30) or red wine vinegar

Garnish

soy sour cream

chopped fresh dill

• •

In a large soup pot, heat oil, and sauté onion until translucent and lightly browned.

Stir in carrots and beets, and sauté another 2 minutes. Add water, lentils, bay leaves, and salt. Bring to a boil, then lower heat and simmer, partially covered, 25–30 minutes. Remove bay leaves. Let soup cool slightly, then purée in small batches in a blender. Stir in vinegar after all the puréed soup has been returned to the pot. Rewarm if necessary before serving. Garnish each serving with a dollop of soy sour cream and some chopped dill.

Loving Lentil

6–8 SERVINGS

2 cups brown or green lentils

¼ cup olive oil

2 medium onions, finely chopped

6 garlic cloves, sliced

2 carrots, diced

1 red bell pepper, diced

6 cups water

1 Tbsp sea salt

½ tsp black pepper

2–3 Tbsp umeboshi or red wine vinegar

¼ cup fresh chopped parsley

....

Rinse lentils with cool water in a strainer. Heat oil in a large soup pot, and sauté onions and garlic until transparent and lightly browned. Add carrots and bell pepper, and sauté another minute or two. Add water, lentils, salt, and pepper. Bring to a boil, then reduce heat and simmer, partially covered, for 25 minutes, stirring occasionally. Remove from flame and add vinegar. Garnish servings with fresh chopped parsley.

Nacho Gazpacho

6–8 SERVINGS

2 corn tortillas

¼ cup apple cider vinegar

2 garlic cloves, sliced

¼ cup olive oil

1 large cucumber, peeled, seeded, and chopped

1 red bell pepper, diced

6 large tomatoes, finely chopped

1 avocado, cut into ¼-inch cubes

1 cup cold water

1–2 Tbsp canned chipotle juice

2 tsp sea salt

½ tsp black pepper

2 cups corn tortilla chips

½ cup fresh cilantro leaves

· ·

Tear corn tortillas into 1- or 2-inch pieces, and purée in a blender with vinegar, garlic, and olive oil. In a large bowl, combine remaining ingredients, then stir in tortilla mixture. Refrigerate and serve chilled. Garnish each serving with a few corn tortilla chips and fresh cilantro.

Atomic Split Pea

6–8 SERVINGS

1½ cups yellow split peas

1 onion, chopped

2 medium carrots, chopped

2 Tbsp olive or sunflower oil

1 cup diced seitan, ¼-inch cubes

8 cups water

1 Tbsp sea salt

½ tsp black pepper

1 tsp fresh chopped rosemary

1 cup Country Croutons (page 92)

¼ cup finely chopped chives or green onions

....

In a large soup pot, heat oil and sauté onions until transparent and lightly browned. Add carrot and seitan, and sauté another 1–2 minutes. While mixture is sautéing, place split peas in a colander and rinse. Add split peas, water, salt, and pepper to pot and simmer, partially covered, 1 hour. Garnish each serving with a touch of rosemary, a few Country Croutons, and chopped chives or green onion.

VARIATIONS

• *Substitute a vegetarian ham-style meat for seitan. Yves brand makes a good Canadian Veggie Bacon, and Asian markets have some good ham-style products.*
• *Substitute 2–3 tablespoons vegetarian bacon bits for seitan.*

Caldo Verde (Portuguese Greens Soup)

Many Portuguese households have a pot of this nutritious greens soup simmering on the stove daily. This recipe makes quite a bit, so cook up a batch and give some to friends—it's the perfect thoughtful thing to do!

1 bunch fresh kale or collards

1 bunch fresh spinach

¼ cup olive oil

2 medium onions, chopped

4 garlic cloves, sliced

2 medium potatoes, scrubbed and chopped into ½-inch cubes

8 cups water

1½ Tbsp sea salt

Wash greens thoroughly and slice into ⅛-inch strips. Heat olive oil in a large soup pot, and sauté onions and garlic until translucent and lightly browned. Add potatoes and sauté another 5 minutes. Add greens, water, and salt. Simmer, uncovered, 25–30 minutes. Let cool slightly, then purée half of mixture and return to pot. Rewarm if necessary before serving.

Cravin' Corn Chowder

4–6 SERVINGS

SERVING SUGGESTION

Garnish each serving with a fresh sprig of thyme or some chopped fresh parsley.

VARIATION

Purée only half of soup for a chunky chowder version.

¼ cup olive oil

1 onion, chopped

3 cups corn kernels, fresh or frozen (2 cups for soup; save 1 cup for garnish)

2 medium potatoes, cut into 1-inch cubes

1 Tbsp sea salt

½ tsp black pepper

1½ tsp dried thyme

6 cups water

....

Heat olive oil in a large saucepan, and sauté onion until transparent and lightly browned. Stir in 2 cups corn kernels, potatoes, and seasonings. Add 6 cups water, and simmer 20–25 minutes. Remove from heat and let cool slightly. Then purée in a blender. Pour purée back into pot, and add remaining 1 cup of whole corn kernels. Rewarm if needed if you are serving immediately.

Black Bean Soup with Masa Balls

4–6 SERVINGS

1 cup uncooked black beans

4 cups water for soaking

2–3 Tbsp olive or sunflower oil

1 large onion, chopped

5 garlic cloves, sliced

1 Tbsp ground cumin

½ tsp ground coriander

6 cups water

1 canned chipotle chili

2–3 bay leaves

1 cup fresh or frozen corn kernels

1 recipe for Masa Balls (page 160)

½ cup fresh cilantro leaves

¼ cup Black Creek Ranch Dressing (page 113), optional

Soak black beans in 4 cups water for 6 hours or overnight. You could substitute 2 cups canned beans if you like.

Heat olive oil in a large soup pot, and sauté onions and garlic until transparent and lightly browned. Add cumin and coriander, and sauté 1 minute. Add beans with soak liquid, water, and bay leaves. Bring to a boil and simmer, partially covered, for 1½ hours. Add corn kernels and chipotle, and simmer for another 15 minutes. Remove chipotle chili when done, as it will be too spicy to bite into. Garnish each serving with a few Masa Balls, fresh cilantro, and a drizzle of Black Creek Ranch Dressing.

Masa Balls

1 cup cornmeal

1 tsp sea salt

¼ tsp baking powder

1 tsp olive or sunflower oil

¼ cup water

¼ cup sunflower or safflower oil for sautéing

· ·

Mix dry ingredients together in a small bowl. Mix in olive oil and water. Form into small balls, ½ to ¾ inches in diameter. Heat ¼ cup oil in a skillet and sauté Masa Balls until browned and slightly crispy. Remove and place on plate with paper towel to drain excess oil.

OUCH!

Once at the restaurant, when I made the Black Bean Soup, I forgot to remove the whole chipotle chili that flavors the dish. Chipotles resemble sun-dried tomatoes when cooked in a soup, and that is exactly what one customer thought it was when she bit into it. Well, I'll never do that again! There's not much you can do for a person immediately when that happens, let alone the next morning! Thank goodness she is one of the nicest and most regular, and I must add forgiving, customers we have.

Whirled Peas

The French call this soup Potage Saint-Germain, but I like to call it Whirled Peas because of the global ideal implied.

2–3 Tbsp olive oil

6 shallots, peeled and sliced

2 cups fresh or frozen green peas

5 cups water

1 Tbsp sea salt

1 Tbsp herbs de Provence

¼ tsp white pepper

1 cup Country Croutons (page 92)

¼ cup finely chopped chives or green onions

Heat olive oil in a soup pot and sauté shallots until translucent and lightly browned. Add peas, water, and seasonings. Simmer 25–30 minutes. Let cool slightly, and purée in blender. Garnish servings with Country Croutons and chopped chives or green onions.

Fresh Asparagus Soup

∙∙

Follow directions for Whirled Peas soup (page 161), substituting for the green peas two large bunches of fresh asparagus and one medium peeled potato chopped into ½-inch cubes.

To prepare asparagus spears: Snap off end as low as possible where break happens naturally. This should eliminate the hard stringy portion. Cut off the tips and set aside. Cut the stems into ½-inch pieces. After soup has been puréed, return it to the pot and add asparagus tips. Simmer another 10 minutes before serving. Garnish as for Whirled Peas.

Butternut Squash and Lemon Grass Bisque

6–8 SERVINGS

PEELING SQUASH

When peeling large winter squash, it's best to use a T-shaped style of vegetable peeler, which has the peeler portion perpendicular to the handle. This makes peeling the larger and harder-skinned squashes much easier.

1 medium butternut squash

2 onions, chopped

¼ cup olive or sunflower oil

8 cups water

1 Tbsp sea salt

1 large (12-inch) stalk lemon grass

1 cup dried cranberries

½ cup chopped chives or green onions

Peel squash, remove seeds, and chop into 1-inch cubes. Heat olive oil in a large soup pot, and sauté onion until translucent and lightly browned. Add squash, water, and sea salt. Bring to a boil, then lower heat and simmer 25 minutes. Cool slightly, and purée in batches in a blender. Return purée to pot. Score lemon grass stalk lengthwise in quarters and place in soup. Turn heat to low and simmer at least 10 minutes with lemon grass until some of the flavor is released. The longer it stays in, the more flavor! Remove the lemon grass stalk before serving. Garnish soup servings with dried cranberries and chopped chives or green onions.

Manilow's Minestrone

6–8 SERVINGS

When Barry Manilow moved to Palm Springs he became a customer. It's a pleasure to be around someone who loves what he does, singing to bring people pleasure. Barry defines the word "gentleman." This recipe is dedicated to all the wonderful musicians who sing from their hearts for the world to enjoy—and to Barry himself, who believes that if you do what you love, "one voice" can make a difference. It certainly is a soothing soup to enjoy when traveling and singing on the road. And it's hearty enough to be used as a main meal.

¼ cup olive oil
1 onion, chopped
6 garlic cloves, sliced
2 medium carrots, diced
1 red bell pepper, diced
1 cup finely shredded green cabbage
¼ cup minced celery
1 tsp dried thyme
½ tsp dried oregano
¼ cup soy sauce
5 cups water
28-oz can chopped or crushed peeled tomatoes
1 cup cooked garbanzo beans
1 cup cooked kidney beans
1 medium zucchini, diced
½ tsp sea salt
¼ tsp black pepper
1 cup cooked alphabet pasta
1 cup chopped fresh parsley

Heat olive oil in a large soup pot, and sauté onion and garlic until transparent and lightly browned. Add carrots, bell pepper, cabbage, celery, thyme, and oregano, and sauté another 3–4 minutes. Stir in soy sauce and water, tomatoes, cooked beans, zucchini, sea salt, and black pepper, and simmer 20–25 minutes. Add pasta and chopped parsley just before serving.

SERVING SUGGESTIONS

• *Ladle soup over a scoopful of cooked grain for a really hearty meal, or serve with Roasted Garlic Cloves (page 86) on toasted sourdough bread.*
• *Sprinkle with some nondairy parmesan before serving.*

VARIATIONS

• *Substitute or add any other vegetables you like or have in the refrigerator waiting to be used.*
• *In place of the ¼ cup soy sauce plus 5 cups water, use 5¼ cups seitan broth (leftover after you've made seitan).*
• *Add 1½ cups chopped seitan for a thicker, meatier version.*

salads

Many people still incorrectly think that salads are all that vegetarians eat. Our salad section at Native Foods dispels the myth that a salad is "just lettuce." By combining grains, beans, and some of the fun meat alternatives with scrumptious dressings, you will find that the thoughts of salads past "don't live here anymore." Dorothy, it isn't rabbit food anymore!

Mecca Azteca Salad

4 SERVINGS

We've come a long way from the "secretary's lunch" of the 1980s, consisting of a lettuce salad and a container of yogurt. With the addition of a grain, pumpkin seeds, and currants, this salad is a complete, hearty, and satisfying meal.

The Mecca Azteca Salad using deglet noor dates was among the nine finalists of more than one hundred entries in the 2002 Date Chef Competition at the Lodge in Rancho Mirage, California, sponsored by the California Date Board.

1 cup chopped tomato
1 cup peeled and chopped cucumber
1 cup chopped jicama
1 cup chopped avocado
½ cup chopped red onion
2 Tbsp lemon juice
½ tsp sea salt
2 cups mixed salad greens
4 cups cooked quinoa, cooled (see table on page 62)
1 cup Mango Lime Vinaigrette (page 107)

Garnish
½ cup fresh cilantro leaves
4 Tbsp roasted pumpkin seeds
4 Tbsp currants, raisins, or chopped dates
4 slices fresh mango
1 tsp chipotle powder or cayenne pepper (optional)

In a bowl, combine tomato, cucumber, jicama, avocado, and red onion. Toss with lemon juice and sea salt. Divide salad greens on four plates or bowls. Top each with 1 cup of cooked quinoa. On each serving, drizzle quinoa with about 2 tablespoons of the Mango Lime Vinaigrette. On each serving, place one-quarter of the tomato mixture on top of the quinoa. Drizzle a bit more Mango Lime Vinaigrette on top of the tomato mixture on each serving. Garnish each serving with cilantro leaves, pumpkin seeds, currants, fresh mango slice, and chipotle powder.

Warm and Wild Mushroom Salad

4 SERVINGS

This salad is part warm and part cold, like a warm kiss on a cold night—a romantic salad. It also is a brothy salad, so you can dip the bread in it.

VARIATION

Mushrooms may be tossed with oil and salt and then grilled before being added to broth for an added flavor boost.

SERVING SUGGESTION

This salad needs to be served with a warm crusty bread that you can dip and soak in the broth that becomes mixed with the vinaigrette and infused with those great mushroom flavors. With this dish you can't be shy about dipping.

2–3 Tbsp olive or sunflower oil

½ lb oyster mushrooms

½ lb Portobello mushrooms, sliced

¼ tsp sea salt

1 cup Simple Deglaze (page 65)

¼ cup sake (rice wine)

8 cups mixed baby lettuce greens

4 Tbsp Basic Balsamic Vinaigrette (page 104)

4 Tbsp chopped fresh parsley

Separate the oyster mushrooms if in clusters and remove the hard stems.

Heat olive oil in a skillet and sauté oyster and Portobello mushrooms until nicely browned. Sprinkle with salt and remove from skillet.

To the same skillet, add Simple Deglaze and sake, and bring to a boil. Return mushrooms to skillet and simmer for about 1 minute, then remove from flame.

Arrange mixed baby greens in bowls or plates deep enough to hold some broth. Drizzle 1 tablespoon Basic Balsamic Vinaigrette over each plate of greens. Portion and arrange mushrooms on top of greens. Portion broth over each serving. Garnish with fresh chopped parsley.

California Caesar

4 SERVINGS

1 head romaine lettuce

½ cup Caesar's Vegan dressing (page 112)

1 cup Country Croutons (page 92)

1 avocado, sliced

4 lemon slices

....

Slice romaine head lengthwise in quarters. Remove base and chop lettuce into 1-inch pieces. Place in a mixing bowl and toss with Caesar's Vegan dressing and croutons. Arrange avocado slices with salad on individual plates or in a serving bowl, and garnish with lemon slices.

VARIATIONS

• *Serve with sliced or chopped tempeh or soy brests (see pages 73 and 76).*
• *Serve with blackened tempeh or blackened soy brests (see page 44).*

Soy Amigo

4 SERVINGS

Here's a reminder of why soy is your friend.

2 cups finely shredded romaine lettuce

2 cups finely shredded green cabbage

¼ cup Basic Balsamic Vinaigrette (page 104)

2 cups Taco Meat (page 74)

2½ cups Salsa Fresca (page 121)

½ cup Black Creek Ranch Dressing (page 113)

1 cup corn tortilla chips

½ cup loosely packed fresh cilantro leaves

½ cup chopped green onions

½ cup sliced black olives

½ cup fresh or defrosted frozen corn kernels

1 avocado, sliced

Divide equal amounts of lettuce and cabbage on four plates or serving bowls. Drizzle each with about two teaspoons of Basic Balsamic Vinaigrette. Place equal portions of Taco Meat and then Salsa Fresca on top of lettuce and cabbage. Drizzle each with about 1½ tablespoons of Black Creek Ranch Dressing. Garnish with tortilla chips, cilantro, green onions, olives, and corn. Arrange avocado slices around each portion. Call your amigos to lunch!

Tanya's Tempeh Salad

4 SERVINGS

I didn't name this dish after myself; it just kind of happened on its own, probably because of my unceasing devotion to this fabulous food.

8 cups mixed baby lettuce greens or salad greens of choice

4 cups cooked brown, basmati, or jasmine rice

½ cup Basic Balsamic Vinaigrette (page 104)

1½ cups Tempeh Pâté (page 138)

1 cup grated carrot

1 cup sunflower sprouts

½ cup chopped green onions

Arrange salad greens on four plates or bowls. Top each with 1 cup brown rice. Drizzle about 1½ tablespoons of Basic Balsamic Vinaigrette over rice and greens. Top with equal portions of tempeh pâté. Garnish circumference of each plate with grated carrot and sunflower sprouts. Toss green onions on top of each portion.

Simple Pleasures

4 SERVINGS

Quick, healing, and healthy, macrobiotic-style. Just chew slowly. This can be eaten warm or chilled, depending on the season.

4 cups cooked barley, or other grain of choice

6 cups steamed or blanched mixed veggies

2 cups cooked adzuki beans, or other bean of choice

4 Tbsp umeboshi vinegar

4 tsp Gomasio (page 95)

....

Spoon 1 cup of barley in each of four bowls. Portion out the veggies and then beans into each bowl. Sprinkle each with umeboshi vinegar and Gomasio.

José y Jesus' Jicama Salad

4–6 SERVINGS

1 small jicama, peeled and chopped

1 tomato, chopped

1 cucumber, peeled, seeded, and chopped

1 bunch green onions, chopped

¼ cup olive or sunflower oil

¼ cup lime juice

1 garlic clove, minced

¼ cup chopped fresh cilantro leaves

½ tsp sea salt

¼ tsp chipotle powder, cayenne pepper, or hot sauce (optional)

....

In a bowl, mix together jicama, tomato, cucumber, and green onions. In a separate small bowl, mix together the olive oil, lime juice, garlic, cilantro, salt, and the chipotle powder. Pour olive oil and lime juice mixture over vegetables and toss

VARIATION

Substitute 1 cup chopped papaya for tomato.

Iron Yam

6 SERVINGS

This dish will make you feel as strong and healthy as the Iron Man triathlon guys and gals.

VARIATION

• *Substitute any flavor dressing or marinade for the Balsamic Vinaigrette.*
• *Prepare as above but chill all the ingredients before assembling salads when serving during the warmer weather months.*

3 medium yams
1 recipe Basic Tofu Marinade (page 80)
14–16 oz firm Chinese-style tofu (not silken), sliced
5–6 cups steamed mixed veggies
6 cups mixed baby lettuce greens
½ cup Basic Balsamic Vinaigrette (page 104)
6 Tbsp Caramelized Onions (page 102)
¼ cup fresh chopped parsley
3–4 Tbsp Brunoise-cut red bell pepper (optional)

Preheat oven to 375°F. Wash and scrub yams and bake for one hour.

Prepare Basic Tofu Marinade, marinate tofu slices for at least 20 minutes, and bake tofu with marinade for 20 minutes at 375°F. Coordinate so you bake the tofu with the yams at the end of their baking time. That's called "feeding two birds with one seed." Brilliant!

Steam veggies toward end of baking time for tofu and yams, or prepare earlier and rewarm just before serving.

Arrange salad greens on six plates or bowls. Top with steamed veggies.

Cut baked yams in half lengthwise, and place one half with flesh exposed on top for color. Put 1 tablespoon of Caramelized Onions on top of each yam half.

Cut tofu slices into triangles and place around circumference of dish.

Drizzle entire dish with Basic Balsamic Vinaigrette. Garnish with chopped parsley and Brunoise-cut red bell pepper.

Native Chop Chop

4 SERVINGS

4 cups chopped romaine lettuce

4 cups steamed mixed veggies, chilled and diced

1 cup diced seitan

1 cup diced tomato

½ cup chopped green onion

½ cup chopped cilantro leaves

½ cup Sesame Orange Vinaigrette (page 110)

4 Tbsp toasted sesame seeds

....

In a large bowl, toss all ingredients together except sesame seeds. Serve in a bowl or individual plates, garnished with sesame seeds.

VARIATION

Use grilled or roasted mixed vegetables instead of steamed.

Bye Bye Barnum Black Bean Salad

4 SERVINGS

This one the elephants had me name (check out www.elephants.com to find out why they should be in sanctuaries, not circuses). It's had a few different names on the menu throughout the years. I served this salad at my first restaurant over thirteen years ago, and it's been a best-seller every time!

4–5 cups warm cooked black beans

1 cup very thinly sliced red onions

½ cup Basic Balsamic Vinaigrette (page 104)

6 cups mixed baby lettuce or salad greens of choice

2 cups warm cooked brown rice

1 cup Salsa Fresca (page 121)

1 cup corn tortilla chips

½ cup loosely packed fresh cilantro leaves

½ cup fresh or defrosted frozen corn kernels

In a bowl, toss black beans with red onions and ¼ cup of the Balsamic Vinaigrette. Divide the lettuce into four plates or bowls. Drizzle the other ¼ cup of Balsamic Vinaigrette over the greens. Top each plate of greens with ½ cup brown rice. Spoon a quarter of the bean mixture over rice in each plate. Top each with Salsa Fresca. Garnish with tortilla chips, fresh cilantro, and corn kernels.

VARIATION

Use white beans; substitute Italian Salsa (page 120) for Salsa Fresca; use fresh basil instead of cilantro; and omit corn chips.

Perestroika (Russian Salad)

6 SERVINGS

The word *perestroika* actually means "rebuilding the system." I don't know how well this salad works politically, but healthwise it's great! I grew up loving beets because of this salad.

2 medium Yukon gold potatoes, boiled, peeled, and chopped

3 medium beets, boiled, peeled, and chopped

2 medium carrots, chopped and blanched

1 cup chopped fresh green beans, blanched

1 cup fresh or frozen green peas (if fresh, need to blanch)

1 cup chopped fresh dill

1 cup Basic Balsamic Vinaigrette

½ tsp sea salt

Garnish

½ cup Quick Tofu Egg (page 178)

¼ cup fresh dill sprigs

¼ cup Brunoise-cut red bell pepper (see page 45)

. . . .

In a large bowl, toss the vegetables, chopped dill, Balsamic Vinaigrette, and sea salt together. Divide into serving portions, and garnish each with 1 tablespoon of Quick Tofu Egg, fresh dill sprigs, and chopped red bell pepper.

Quick Tofu Egg

½ CUP

1 tsp sunflower oil

4 oz tofu, any style or texture, crumbled

2 pinches turmeric

¼ tsp sea salt

TOFU EGG SALAD

Add 1 teaspoon nondairy mayonnaise and 1 teaspoon chopped red onion to Quick Tofu Egg for a tofu egg salad.

Heat oil in a small skillet and add crumbled tofu, turmeric, and sea salt. Sauté 1 or 2 minutes until color is uniform. Let cool.

Chinese "Save the Chicken" Salad

4 SERVINGS

Dedicated to the chickens of China.

4 sautéed or grilled soy brests (page 77)

6 cups chopped romaine lettuce

4 cups finely shredded cabbage

2 cups cooked jasmine rice, cooled

1½ cups fresh or defrosted frozen corn kernels

1 cup chopped green onion

1 cup Sesame Orange Vinaigrette (page 110)

1 cup loosely packed fresh cilantro leaves

1 cup Brunoise-cut red bell pepper (see page 45)

Chop or slice the sautéed or grilled soy brests. Place in a bowl with the romaine, cabbage, rice, corn, and green onion. Add Sesame Orange Vinaigrette and toss well. Divide salad into four bowls, and top with sesame seeds, cilantro leaves, and chopped red bell pepper.

Fellini's Dream

4 SERVINGS

I'd love to see Sophia Loren
eating this one day!

2 cups mixed baby lettuce greens

4 cups cooked rigatoni or penne pasta, cooled

1 cup Italian Salsa (page 120)

½ cup chopped sun-dried tomatoes

12 oz artichoke hearts, canned or bottled

½ cup Basic Balsamic Vinaigrette (page 104)

½ cup toasted pine nuts

two 2½ –3 oz sautéed tempeh patties, blackened
(page 44) and chopped

4 Tbsp fresh basil chiffonade (page 45)

Reconstitute the dried tomatoes by soaking them in enough
hot water to cover for about 15 minutes, until soft; then
drain. In a bowl, toss lettuce, pasta, Italian Salsa, reconstituted sun-dried tomatoes, and artichoke hearts with
Balsamic Vinaigrette. Portion salad onto four plates, and
top with pine nuts and chopped tempeh. Garnish with
fresh basil chiffonade.

Gorgeous Greek

4 SERVINGS

Not that any Greek I know would only cook for four, so if Greeks are coming for dinner, increase the recipe proportions!

1 cup chopped tomato

1 cup peeled and chopped cucumber

1 cup chopped red bell pepper

½ cup chopped red onion

½ cup pitted Kalamata olives

½ cup Greek Lemon Garlic Dressing (page 106)

¼ tsp dried oregano

¼ tsp sea salt

1½ cups Tofu Feta (page 99)

½ cup chopped fresh parsley

....

In a bowl, combine all ingredients except Tofu Feta and fresh parsley. Portion into four bowls, and top each with Tofu Feta and chopped parsley.

Farrah's Fattoush

4 SERVINGS

Fattoush is a Middle Eastern bread salad. It's a good way to use slightly dried good bread. It is similar to the Gorgeous Greek salad, with variations.

Make the recipe for the Gorgeous Greek Salad (page 181) with the following variations:

Add 2 cups of day-old French or other rustic type of bread that has been cut into 1-inch cubes. You can also use pita bread torn into pieces. Increase Greek Lemon Garlic Dressing to ¾ cup. Add 1 cup cooked garbanzo beans, or top each salad with 2 tablespoons hummus, or both! In addition to parsley for garnish, sprinkle each serving with ¼ teaspoon sumac, a dried tangy-flavored spice (made from a Mediterranean berry) available in the import section of grocery stores or Middle Eastern markets.

Fleetwood Macaroni Salad

4–6 SERVINGS

2 cups cooked elbow macaroni

1 cup fresh or defrosted frozen corn kernels

½ cup chopped celery

½ cup chopped carrot

½ cucumber, peeled, seeded and cut into quarters

½ cup chopped red bell pepper

¼ cup chopped parsley

¼ cup chopped chives or green onions

¼ cup lemon juice

1 cup vegan mayonnaise

1½ tsp sea salt

½ tsp pepper

....

Toss all ingredients together, and put on some hits from the '70s.

VARIATION

Add 2 teaspoons curry powder. For an extra-spicy touch, add an additional ¼ teaspoon cayenne powder.

Lemon Potato Salad

8 SERVINGS

2 lbs boiled Yukon gold or other potatoes

1 cup finely chopped parsley

¾ cup olive oil

½ cup fresh lemon juice

1 red onion, thinly sliced

1½ tsp sea salt

½ tsp pepper

....

Peel cooled potatoes and cut into 1-inch cubes. Place in a bowl with the other ingredients and toss well.

Wheat Berry Waldorf Salad

6 SERVINGS

A new spin on a classic American salad invented in the 1890s at the Waldorf Astoria Hotel in New York. Originally made of only apples, celery, and egg mayonnaise, the Waldorf salad today typically includes raisins and walnuts. Our version, with wheat berries and dried cranberries, makes a nice dish to serve during the fall and winter holidays.

2 medium Granny Smith apples

2 stalks celery, minced

2 cups cooked wheat berries (see page 62)

1 cup dried cranberries

3/4 cup vegan mayonnaise

1/4 cup lemon juice

1/4 cup maple syrup

1/4 tsp sea salt

• •

Remove core and seeds from apples, and chop into 1/2-inch pieces. If the apples are organic, I like leaving the peel on, but the choice is yours. Place chopped apples in a bowl with the rest of the ingredients, and mix together well.

VARIATIONS

• *Add 1 cup chopped walnuts, cashews, or hazelnuts.*
• *Substitute chopped dried apricots for cranberries.*
• *Use spelt berries in place of wheat berries if you're wheat-intolerant.*

Watermelon Chill

You may think the onion seems unusual in this recipe, but trust me. The key is to really slice the onion as thin as possible, maybe use a mandolin or hand-type slicer. This is my favorite thing to eat on a hot summer day, and we have a lot of those in Palm Springs!

4 cups chopped watermelon, cut into 1-inch cubes.

½ small red onion, *very* thinly sliced

¼ cup raspberry vinegar (I use an imported French brand)

....

Toss all together in bowl. Keep chilled until ready to serve. Don't throw away the juice—it's the best part!

TuNO

6 SERVINGS

12 oz frozen Tuno

½ cup vegan mayonnaise

⅓ cup diced celery

½ cup chopped red onion

¼ tsp black pepper

SERVING SUGGESTION

Substitute this recipe for tempeh salad in the Palm Springs Wrap or Tanya's Tempeh Salad (pages 196 and 171).

Defrost the Tuno. Remove it from the package and place it in a strainer to drain the excess liquid. Place in a bowl and mix with the rest of the ingredients.

NO TUNA!

"Tuno" is the brand name of a product manufactured by Worthington Foods. The version I prefer is the frozen style, as opposed to the canned. Tuno is soy-based and quite a trip to taste. The flavor and texture is very much like tuna, the beloved fish that swim below the dolphins in the oceans of the world, and may they continue to swim with the dolphins . . . may we all! The European community is engaging in serious discussions about the fishing situation as the fish stocks over the last thirty years have plummeted. Cod, whiting, and haddock are now endangered. Eat Tuno!

Thai Slaw

4–6 SERVINGS

At our restaurants, we serve this slaw with most of our sandwiches instead of the typical American recipe that's loaded with egg mayonnaise and white sugar.

6 cups finely shredded green cabbage

2 cups finely shredded red cabbage

1 cup shredded carrot

1 cup roasted, unsalted peanuts

½ cup chopped green onion

¾ cup Sesame Orange Vinaigrette (page 110)

¼ tsp sea salt

¼ tsp crushed red chilies (optional)

....

Mix all ingredients together in a large bowl.

VARIATIONS

• *Add 1 cup chopped fresh pineapple or mango to make it muy tropical.*
• *Garnish with roasted sesame seeds.*

Quinoa Tabouli

4 SERVINGS

A variation on the traditional Middle Eastern salad usually made with bulghur wheat (which you can also try).

2 cups cooked quinoa
½ cup finely chopped parsley
¼ cup finely chopped fresh mint
4 green onions, finely chopped
1 tomato, finely chopped
⅓ cup Greek Lemon Garlic Dressing (page 106)
   romaine lettuce leaves

. . . .

In a large bowl, toss all ingredients except romaine leaves together well. Let chill. Serve individual portions on lettuce leaves.

SERVING SUGGESTION

Serve with Harry's Hummus (page 136), Gorgeous Greek Salad (page 181), and pita bread.

sandwiches, wraps, and burritos

*T*his is the section of our menu where Native Foods added some "normalcy" for both vegans and meat-eaters. In general, the sandwich menu is the most popular in restaurants across the nation. It's been a pleasure giving everyone some popular options!

'70s Delight

I was in high school when I had my first avocado sandwich, and yes, it was in the '70s. It was soon after I had become a vegetarian, and this sandwich became my staple for many years. It's still a classic menu item reminiscent of the era when health food and vegetarianism started moving fashionably forward. . . . Is it mainstream yet?

SERVING SUGGESTION

Serve with Fleetwood Macaroni Salad (page 183) and some granola with soy yogurt for a flashback luncheon.

2 slices sprouted wheat bread

2 Tbsp Harry's Hummus (page 136)

½ tsp vegan mayonnaise

2 Tbsp grated carrot

¼ avocado, sliced
handful sunflower or alfalfa sprouts

¼ tsp Gomasio (page 95) or 2 pinches sea salt

1 slice red onion

2 slices tomato

....

Spread mayonnaise on one slice of bread and hummus on the other. On the hummus slice, begin assembling: first carrot, then sliced avocado, and sprouts. Sprinkle on Gomasio or sea salt, then place red onion and tomato. Top with other bread slice.

VARIATIONS

• *Use Thousand Island Dressing (page 111) instead of mayonnaise and/or hummus.*
• *Add 2 tablespoons Tofu Ricotta (page 98).*

TuNO Salad Sandwich

4 SANDWICHES

This one really cuts to the net; need I say it's dolphin- and tuna-safe?

Eat TuNO Salad Sandwiches on a fishing boat in front of people who like to fish for tuna, and give them a bite!

8 slices sprouted wheat bread
1½ cups TuNO Salad (page 187)
4 Tbsp Tartar Sauce (page 129) or vegan mayonnaise
½ cup grated carrot
4 leaves romaine lettuce
8 slices tomato

For each sandwich, spread about one-quarter of the TuNO Salad on one slice of bread and 1 tablespoon Tartar Sauce on the other. Arrange some grated carrot, 1 romaine leaf, and 2 tomato slices on top of TuNO. Top with bread slice spread with Tartar Sauce.

VARIATION

Substitute Tanya's Tempeh Salad (page 171) for TuNO.

Hot Italian

4 SANDWICHES

Everyone needs a hot Italian at least once in their life!

2–3 Tbsp olive or sunflower oil

1 cup sliced onion

¼ tsp fennel seeds

1 cup sliced red bell pepper

1 cup sliced green bell pepper

½ lb seitan, sliced

1 cup sliced mushrooms

¼ tsp sea salt

4 Italian or hoagie rolls

4 Tbsp Basic Balsamic Vinaigrette (page 104)

1 cup Simple Marinara (page 118), warmed

2 oz Native Ch'i's (nondairy cheese, page 97)

....

Heat olive oil in a skillet and sauté sliced onion with fennel seeds until onion is transparent and lightly browned. Add bell peppers, seitan, mushrooms, and salt, and sauté until peppers are lightly browned, another 2–3 minutes. Slice rolls in half lengthwise, not quite slicing all the way through. Drizzle each roll with 1 tablespoon Balsamic Vinaigrette. Portion one-quarter of the sautéed mixture in each roll, then top with Simple Marinara and Native Ch'i's.

Philly Peppersteak

4 SANDWICHES

This we recommend for members of the Carnivore Culture Club, and they don't regret it!

¼ cup + 2 Tbsp olive or sunflower oil

3 peeled shallots, thinly sliced

1 lb seitan, sliced

½ cup Seitan Broth (page 70) or Simple Deglaze (page 65)

1 oz cognac or brandy (optional)

1 cup sliced red bell pepper

1 cup sliced green bell pepper

1 cup sliced mushrooms

¼ tsp sea salt

4 Italian or hoagie rolls

4 Tbsp Basic Balsamic Vinaigrette (page 104)

2 Tbsp Native Ch'i's (nondairy cheese, page 97)

1 cup shredded romaine lettuce

....

Heat ¼ cup oil in a skillet and sauté shallots until transparent; then add seitan slices and sauté until lightly browned, about 2–3 minutes. Add Seitan Broth or Simple Deglaze and stir. Add cognac and lightly tilt pan so that broth is exposed to flame, or use a long-handled lighter and place flame close to broth. Don't be surprised when a flame arises, as you have just "flambéed"! Let simmer until most of the liquid is reduced.

In another skillet, heat 2 Tbsp of oil and sauté bell peppers until lightly browned; then add mushrooms and salt, and sauté another 2–3 minutes.

Slice rolls in half lengthwise, not quite slicing all the way through. Drizzle each roll with 1 tablespoon Balsamic Vinaigrette. Portion one-quarter of the seitan and bell pepper mixture in each roll, then top with Native Ch'i's and shredded romaine lettuce.

Palm Springs Wrap (Tempeh Salad Wrap)

1 WRAP

1 soft lavosh flatbread

½ cup cooked jasmine rice

½ cup Tempeh Pâté (page 138)

¼ cup shredded carrot

¼ cup chopped tomato

   handful sunflower or alfalfa sprouts

1 Tbsp Basic Balsamic Vinaigrette (page 104)

Place lavosh flatbread on a flat surface. Spread rice along bottom third of bread, leaving about a 2-inch margin from the very bottom. Spread tempeh over rice, then carrot, chopped tomato, and sprouts. Drizzle Balsamic Vinaigrette over sprouts. Fold a 2-inch margin over the food, and roll it inside as tight as possible. Slice in half on a diagonal.

VARIATION

Substitute a burrito-sized flour tortilla for the lavosh flatbread.

California Caesar Wrap with Tempeh

I WRAP

1 soft lavosh flatbread

½ cup cooked brown rice

1½ cups shredded romaine lettuce

¼ cup Country Croutons (page 92)

¼ cup Caesar's Vegan dressing (page 112)

⅓ cup chopped tomatoes

¼ avocado, sliced

½ tempeh patty (see Tempeh Basic Prep, page 65), sliced

Place lavosh flatbread on a flat surface. Spread rice along the bottom third of the bread, leaving about a 2-inch margin from the very bottom. In a small bowl, toss lettuce with croutons and Caesar dressing. Spread over rice, then top with chopped tomatoes, avocado, and sliced tempeh. Fold a 2-inch margin over the food, and roll it inside as tight as possible. Slice in half on a diagonal.

VARIATIONS

• *Blacken the tempeh patty as described on page 44.*
• *Substitute a sautéed or grilled soy brest for the tempeh.*

Bali Surf Burger

2 BURGERS

Makes two, because you can't eat just one!

CHOOSING BURGER BUNS

I prefer to use hamburger buns made with a mixture of whole wheat and unbleached flour instead of purely whole wheat or sprouted wheat buns. This creates a lighter bread that doesn't take away from the flavor of the food. Use what you prefer, but remember to think "inside the bun."

2 hamburger buns

2 tsp vegan mayonnaise

2 sautéed tempeh patties (see page 65)

2 romaine lettuce leaves

2 slices tomato

2 slices red onion

Lightly warm or toast hamburger buns. Spread each side with ½ teaspoon mayonnaise. On bottom bun, place sautéed tempeh patty topped with lettuce, tomato, and onion.

VARIATIONS

• *My favorite is topping the tempeh patty with 1 tablespoon of warmed Caramelized Onions (page 102).*
• *Try blackening the tempeh patties before assembling the sandwich (see page 44).*
• *Instead of tomato and onion, use Salsa Fresca (page 121) and add sliced avocado or Guacamole (page 147).*
• *Try Caesar's Vegan (page 112) or Thousand Island Dressing (page 111) instead of mayonnaise.*

Ciao Bella Burger

2 BURGERS

VARIATION

Substitute focaccia bread or rolls for hamburger buns.

2 large Portobello mushrooms

3 Tbsp olive or sunflower oil

¼ tsp sea salt

2–3 oz seitan, sliced

2 hamburger buns

2 tsp vegan mayonnaise

2 Tbsp Italian Salsa (page 120)

2 Tbsp Caramelized Onions (page 102)

6 Roasted Garlic Cloves (page 86)

1 tsp Pumpkin Seed Pesto (page 123)

2–4 large fresh basil leaves

....

Clean and slice Portobello mushrooms in ½ inch slices. Heat oil in skillet, add mushrooms and sprinkle with sea salt and sauté to brown both sides. Remove mushrooms from skillet and add seitan to warm, adding a little oil to skillet if necessary. Slightly warm or toast hamburger buns. Spread each side with ½ teaspoon mayonnaise. On bottom bun, portion Portobello mushrooms. Top mushrooms with Italian Salsa, Caramelized Onions, Roasted Garlic Cloves, pesto, and basil leaves. Now chow bella.

Rocket Burger

2 BURGERS

2 large Portobello mushrooms

3 Tbsp olive or sunflower oil

¼ tsp sea salt

2 hamburger buns

2 tsp vegan mayonnaise

2 Tbsp Papa's Yugoslavian Ivar (page 144)

1 cup loosely packed arugula leaves

• •

Clean Portobello mushrooms and cut them into ½-inch slices. Heat oil in a skillet, add mushrooms, sprinkle with sea salt, and sauté to brown both sides. Slightly warm or toast hamburger buns. Spread each side with ½ teaspoon mayonnaise. On bottom bun, portion Portobello mushrooms. Top with ivar and arugula. Take a bite and blast off.

VARIATION

Great served on French rolls or sliced baguettes.

Poltz Burrito

1 BURRITO

The beauty of a burrito is that you can add anything you want and it just keeps getting better. This burrito really rocks hard, as it was created in honor of Steve Poltz, my childhood friend and neighbor turned rock star. The song he co-wrote with Jewel helped propel her to become a household name. Steve would talk about the late-night meaty burritos he would eat on the road, and I thought this was a version that would keep him healthier (I don't think he's tried one yet!). I also thought of Jewel, who announced at one of her shows that she's not a vegetarian and loves her burgers. Maybe one day she'll try this too.

1 flour tortilla, burrito size
½ cup cooked black beans, warmed
½ cup brown rice
2–3 oz seitan, sliced
⅓ cup Flamed Banana Salsa (page 131)
2 Tbsp Salsa Fresca (page 121)
2 Tbsp Guacamole (page 147)

Slightly warm flour tortilla in a dry skillet. Place the tortilla on a flat surface to begin placing ingredients along the bottom third, leaving about a 2-inch margin from the very bottom. Leave clear about 2 inches on each side as well. Spread bottom with black beans, rice, seitan, and Flamed Banana Salsa. Fold in the sides of the tortilla and, while holding the sides in, fold the bottom up over the filling and continue rolling. Top with salsa and guacamole.

VARIATION

Add the guacamole and salsa to the inside of the burrito if you want to take it "to go."

El Bruncho Burrito

4 BURRITOS

4 flour tortillas, burrito size

1 recipe Tofu Scrambler (page 245)

1 recipe In Thyme for Breakfast Potatoes (page 246)

4 oz sliced seitan, warmed

1 cup Baja Enchilada sauce (page 119)

1 cup Salsa Fresca (page 121)

½ cup Guacamole (page 147)

Slightly warm flour tortillas in a dry skillet. Place each tortilla on a flat surface to begin placing ingredients along the bottom third, leaving about a 2-inch margin from the very bottom. Leave clear about 2 inches on each side as well. Spread the bottom with Tofu Scrambler, potatoes, seitan, and enchilada sauce. Top with salsa and guacamole.

Zucchini Rosemary Sandwich

2 SANDWICHES

3 Tbsp olive oil

2 medium zucchini, grated

2 garlic cloves, sliced

¼ tsp sea salt

⅛ tsp black pepper

1 tsp sherry wine vinegar

¼ tsp chopped fresh rosemary

1 tsp soy Parmesan

2 4-inch squares focaccia bread, or focaccia rolls
sliced in half

4 slices tomato

Heat oil in a skillet and sauté zucchini, garlic, and salt until
there is some browning on the skillet bottom. Add sherry
vinegar and stir while scraping bottom of skillet. (This is
deglazing.) Remove from heat and stir in rosemary. Sprinkle
with soy Parmesan. Place zucchini mixture on focaccia
slices, top with tomato slices, and serve warm.

BBQ Love Burger

2 BURGERS

Love is simple.

½ lb seitan, sliced

½ cup Bessie's (Thank-You) BBQ Sauce (page 128)

2 hamburger buns

2 Tbsp Caramelized Onions (page 102)

½ cup loosely packed sunflower sprouts or shredded romaine lettuce

In a skillet, warm seitan with BBQ Sauce. Slightly warm or toast hamburger buns. On bottom half of buns, portion seitan. Top with Caramelized Onions and sprouts.

Tijuana Tacos

8 TACOS

Also known as T.J. Tacos in Southern California. This is one of the original "hooks" for avid carnivores, kids, and Doubting Thomases. This dish is where the term "Cravin' Native" took off from, as one loyal group of customers would come for their weekly fix, and as they walked in would say, "We're cravin' Native!"

8 corn tortillas

1 Tbsp sunflower or safflower oil

1½–2 cups Taco Meat (page 74)

¼ cup Native Ch'i's (nondairy cheese, page 97)

1 cup Salsa Fresca (page 121)

1 cup shredded romaine lettuce

1 cup shredded green cabbage

½ cup Guacamole (page 147)

Lightly brush one side of corn tortillas with oil. Heat a skillet and place each tortilla oiled side down for about 10 seconds until softened, then turn over to warm the other side for another 5 seconds. Keep warm in a tortilla warmer or in foil until ready to assemble.

Have rest of ingredients ready, and begin by placing approximately 2 heaping tablespoons of Taco Meat in each tortilla, followed by Native Ch'i's, salsa, lettuce, and cabbage, topping with a dollop of Guacamole.

SERVING SUGGESTION

Serve with Salsa de Chupacabra (page 100) or your favorite hot sauce.

Korean Tacos

8 SERVINGS

The beautiful landscapes, the vegetarian temple foods, the demilitarized zone, the smells of garlic and ginseng chewing gum in the subway stations, the Kim Chee Museum—this dish was created out of all the great experiences I returned home with from my travels in Korea.

2 Tbsp sunflower or safflower oil

1 tsp toasted sesame oil

2 garlic cloves, sliced

¼ tsp cayenne powder

1 cup textured soy bits, flakes, or granules

1 cup water

¼ cup soy sauce

2 Tbsp rice vinegar

¼ cup Gomasio (page 95)

8–10 leaves romaine lettuce or Napa cabbage

1 cup sliced radishes

1½ cups bean sprouts

1½ cups chopped cucumber (peeled and seeded)

1½ cups Speedy Kim Chee (page 148)

· ·

Heat oils in saucepan and sauté garlic until lightly browned. Add cayenne, textured soy protein, and water. Bring to a boil, then cover and remove from flame. Let sit 10 minutes. Stir in rice vinegar and Gomasio.

Assemble tacos by using romaine or Napa cabbage leaves in place of a tortilla. Fill each leaf with textured soy protein, then top with radishes, bean sprouts, cucumber, and kim chee.

Tuesday's Mediterranean Sandwich

4 SANDWICHES

1 lb firm Chinese-style tofu

½ cup Pumpkin Seed Pesto (page 123)

¼ cup lemon juice

1 medium eggplant, cut into ½-inch rounds

½ tsp sea salt

⅓ cup olive oil

2 medium zucchini, sliced lengthwise into ¼-inch slices

1 red bell pepper

8 slices Kalamata olive bread

4 tsp Basic Balsamic Vinaigrette (page 104)

2 cups loosely packed sunflower or alfalfa sprouts

• •

Drain tofu and cut it into 8 slices. Combine pesto and lemon juice in a baking dish, and lay tofu slices in this marinade for 30 minutes.

In the meantime, sprinkle salt on the eggplant slices and place them in a colander over the sink to "sweat"; this removes potential bitterness. Let drain 10–15 minutes.

Preheat oven to broil setting (500°F). On a cookie sheet or baking dish, place the bell pepper and broil it until the skin is blistered on all sides. Remove it from the oven, let it cool, then peel, remove seeds, and slice into 1-inch strips.

Brush eggplant slices on each side with olive olive oil, place on cookie sheet or baking tray, and broil for about

5 minutes on each side. The eggplant should be very soft all over . . . like butter, as they say.

Brush zucchini slices on each side with olive oil, and broil for 2–3 minutes per side.

Reduce oven temperature to 375°F. Drain excess pesto marinade from tofu and set it aside. Bake the tofu for 20 minutes.

Lightly toast olive bread or warm it in the oven. Spread sides with some of the pesto marinade.

Assemble each sandwich by putting 2 slices of tofu on one slice of bread and topping with eggplant, zucchini, and roasted red bell peppers. Drizzle with Balsamic Vinaigrette and top with sprouts.

A little extra work, but definitely worth the effort.

Bagel No Lox

I BAGEL

1 fresh bagel, sliced in half

2 Tbsp soy cream cheese

4 slices tomato

4 thin slices red onion

1 tsp capers

2 pinches sea salt

freshly ground black pepper

Warm bagel in toaster. Spread halves with soy cream cheese.
Then top with tomato, red onion, capers, salt, and pepper.

sandwiches, wraps, and burritos

Bagel E

1 BAGEL

This recipe uses watercress, which is one of the richest sources of naturally occurring vitamin E.

3 Tbsp tahini

½ cup chopped watercress

1 Tbsp grated onion

½ tsp Gomasio (page 95) or ¼ tsp sea salt

1 fresh bagel, sliced in half

· ·

In a small bowl, combine tahini, watercress, onion, and Gomasio or sea salt. Warm bagel in toaster. Spread tahini mixture on bagel halves.

VARIATION

Try a dollop of the spread on some warm rice.

entrées

*C*hoose one and score! Remember, my life's mission is to open more places for people to dine and be able to "get" good-tasting vegetarian food, and to teach people how to do it themselves. Your mission: to cook and invite friends and family to enjoy a good vegetarian meal so they may be encouraged to eat this way regularly. Basically we are setting each other up to provide a healthy, happy, and humane future for the world. Can you handle a responsibility that's fun and celebratory? In the words of Margaret Mead:

"Never doubt that a thoughtful group of concerned citizens can change the world. Indeed it's the only thing that ever does." Now let's get cookin'!

Totally Stacked Enchiladas

4 SERVINGS

The assembled individual plates of this dish look awesome!

1 large bunch fresh spinach, washed

2–3 Tbsp olive oil

1 medium onion, chopped

½ lb Portobello mushrooms, chopped

½ lb firm Chinese-style tofu (not silken), grated on the large holes of a hand cheese grater

1 cup corn kernels, fresh or frozen

1 tsp sea salt

¼ tsp black pepper

1 dozen corn tortillas

¼ cup sunflower or safflower oil, for warming tortillas

2 cups cooked black beans (see page 52), warmed

2 cups Baja Enchilada sauce (page 119), warmed

⅓ cup Black Creek Ranch Dressing (page 113)

⅓ cup Guacamole (page 147)

Garnish

½ cup fresh cilantro leaves

¼ cup chopped green onion

4 Tbsp Brunoise-cut red bell pepper (see page 45)

¼ cup corn kernels, fresh or frozen

· ·

First, prepare the spinach. Remove root ends and tough stems after washing. Allowing the water that is on the leaves to stay there, place them in a large soup pot. Cover

Instead of spinach, try another leafy green such as steamed chard, kale, or collards.

SERVING SUGGESTIONS

If you like it spicy, serve with Salsa de Chupacabra (page 100). Start the meal with José y Jesus' Jicama Salad (page 173), and finish with Juan's Flan (page 297) or Mexican Hot Chocolate (page 306) for dessert.

the pot and cook over medium heat until leaves are wilted, about 2–3 minutes. (Don't walk away—it happens quickly!) Drain in a colander; then chop.

Heat the olive oil in a large skillet and sauté onions until transparent and lightly browned. Add chopped mushrooms and grated tofu, and sauté for another minute. Stir in corn kernels, salt, and pepper. Remove from heat and keep warm.

Heat another skillet until hot (a cast-iron skillet works well). Lightly brush one side of the tortillas with oil. Place them, oiled side down, in the hot skillet until softened, then flip to the other side for a few seconds. Place warmed tortillas in a tortilla warmer or wrap them in foil to keep warm while you assemble the enchiladas.

To assemble, place one tortilla on a plate, top with a large spoonful of black beans, one-quarter of the steamed spinach, then about 2 tablespoons of enchilada sauce. Top with another corn tortilla, then one-quarter of the grated tofu filling. Top with remaining tortilla. Ladle enchilada sauce over each stack. Drizzle with Black Creek Ranch Dressing and a dollop of Guacamole. Garnish with cilantro, green onion, chopped red bell pepper, and corn kernels.

Gandhi Bowl

SERVES ONE, THEN
THE WORLD

I like integrating the brown
and white rice for this dish,
but you can use any type of
rice or grain you like. No rice
discrimination here.

⅔ cup cooked brown rice

⅔ cup cooked basmati rice

2 cups steamed mixed veggies

¼ cup Gandhi's Curry Sauce (page 117)

1 sautéed tempeh patty, blackened (see page 44)

2 Tbsp dried cranberries

2 Tbsp chopped green onions

Combine rice in a bowl, and top with steamed mixed veggies and sauce. Chop tempeh patty into cubes and put over veggies. Garnish with dried cranberries and green onions.

A GOOD IDEA

When a journalist asked Mahatma Gandhi, "What do you think of Western civilization?" he answered, "I think it would be a good idea."

Tempeh Scaloppine with Shallot Mushroom Gravy

4 SERVINGS

In Italian it's *scaloppine,* in French it's *escalope,* in German it's *Schnitzel.* It's all about getting a thin slice, which can give a whole new taste experience, since ingredients combine with the sauce in different ways, depending on their size and thickness. So this recipe will leave a very different impression than the Bali Surf Burger, for example. It's how you slice it!

Scaloppine also refers to veal with a delicate texture created by pounding with a mallet. Well, I say, why go through all the prep from baby cow to pounding when you can just use tempeh or seitan?

6 sautéed tempeh patties (see page 65), each 2½ –3 oz

1½ cups Shallot Mushroom Gravy (page 125)

¼ cup finely chopped chives or fresh parsley

....

To slice sautéed tempeh, start in the center of the patty and cut toward the end on a diagonal, as thin as you can. Start the second cut ¼ inch away from the first cut but in the same direction and on an angle. One patty of this size should yield 4–5 slices.

Arrange sautéed patties in a fan style on a plate and spoon the warm sauce on top. Garnish with chives or parsley.

SERVING SUGGESTION

Serve with Roasted Garlic Mashed Potatoes (page 258) and a fresh vegetable side dish.

Tempeh Provençale

4 SERVINGS

6 tempeh patties, each 2½–3 oz, sliced scaloppine style (see page 215) and sautéed

¼ cup olive oil

2 tomatoes, chopped

2 garlic cloves, minced

1 cup canned or bottled artichoke hearts, sliced lengthwise

¼ cup sliced Kalamata olives

1 Tbsp capers

1 tsp sea salt

¼ tsp black pepper

½ cup white wine

2 Tbsp chopped parsley

4 slices fresh lemon

• •

Heat olive oil in a skillet and sauté tomatoes and garlic for 2–3 minutes. Add artichokes, olives, capers, salt, and pepper, and sauté another minute. Add white wine and simmer about 3 minutes. Spoon on top of sliced tempeh. Garnish each serving with lemon slice and parsley.

SERVING SUGGESTION

Serve with Roasted Lemon Potatoes (page 260) and Get Yo' Greens with Gomasio (page 259).

Hungarian Goulash

6 SERVINGS

Serve this at Halloween and call it Transylvanian Ghoulash. Invite the Meaty Boys over for dinner—they'll be wowed.

SERVING SUGGESTION

Serve with a crunchy green salad with Basic Balsamic Vinaigrette (page 104) and Garlic Toast (page 87).

⅓ cup olive oil

2 medium onions, finely chopped

4–5 garlic cloves, sliced

1 red bell pepper, finely chopped

1 green bell pepper, finely chopped

1 lb seitan, cut into 1-inch cubes

¼ cup paprika

1½ tsp sea salt

½ tsp black pepper

2 cups water

2 cups canned crushed peeled tomatoes

2 cups canned or bottled sauerkraut, drained

1 lb pasta (fettuccine or rigatoni works well)

Garnish

soy sour cream

chopped fresh dill

....

Heat olive oil in a skillet and sauté onion, garlic, and red and green bell peppers about 3–4 minutes, until lightly browned. Add seitan and paprika, and sauté another 1–2 minutes. Stir in salt and pepper, water, crushed tomatoes, and sauerkraut. Let simmer, partially covered, 25–30 minutes.

Boil the pasta according to package directions. Portion cooked pasta on plates and top with goulash. Garnish each plate with a dollop of soy sour cream and chopped dill.

Oopa Moussaka

8 SERVINGS

I learned this recipe by working with a wonderful Greek lady, Eleni, at the beginning of my restaurant career. Her preference was always to double the amount of olive oil and black pepper! Oopa, Eleni!

SERVING SUGGESTION

Make it a Greek night. Serve with Gorgeous Greek Salad (page 181) and good crusty bread. Finish with Eleni's Baklava with Sambuca Crème (pages 295 and 302)—then you can break plates ... but please recycle.

TIP

Vegan Béchamel Sauce makes a good topping for steamed veggies.

1 medium eggplant

2 medium zucchini

¼ cup olive oil

1 large onion, chopped

4 garlic cloves, sliced

  28-oz can crushed peeled tomatoes

1 tsp dried oregano

2 tsp sea salt

½ tsp black pepper

1 large baking potato

1 Tbsp olive oil for drizzling on top

  chopped fresh parsley for garnish

Vegan Béchamel Sauce

½ cup olive oil

½ cup unbleached flour

⅛ tsp nutmeg

3 cups soy milk

1 Tbsp cornstarch diluted in ½ cup water (or substitute 1 Tbsp kuzu for the cornstarch)

1½ tsp sea salt

Preheat oven to 375°F.

    Cut eggplant lengthwise into ¼-inch slices. Salt the slices and let them "sweat" for 10 minutes.

Yes, we do it even in Palm Springs in the summertime, when you'd think you wouldn't have to! This means gently salting the eggplant slices and letting them sit in a colander in the sink or on a tray. Moisture will extrude, along with some of the eggplant's astringent bitterness.

VARIATION

For a meatlike texture, add 1½ cups Italian Ground Around (page 75) between the eggplant and zucchini layers.

Cut zucchini lengthwise into ¼-inch slices, and set aside.

Heat ¼ cup olive oil in a saucepan, and sauté onion and garlic until onion is transparent and lightly browned. Add crushed tomatoes, oregano, salt, and pepper. Simmer 5–10 minutes.

Lightly oil the bottom of a 13 x 9 x 2–inch baking dish. Peel potato and cut lengthwise into ¼-inch slices. Layer potato slices in bottom of baking dish, and spoon one-third of the tomato sauce over. Then layer eggplant, one-third of tomato sauce, zucchini slices, and finally the rest of the tomato sauce. Drizzle top with olive oil.

Cover with baking dish lid or foil and bake for 1½ hours.

While dish is baking, prepare Vegan Béchamel Sauce: Heat olive oil in a saucepan, and sprinkle in flour and nutmeg, stirring constantly until mixture is lightly browned and a nutty aroma arises. Whisk in soymilk, cornstarch mixture, and salt, stirring until mixture begins to boil; then reduce heat and whisk until thickened.

Remove moussaka from oven and remove cover. Ladle Vegan Béchamel Sauce over top of casserole and put back in oven to bake for another 20–30 minutes, until top is nicely browned. Let sit a half hour before cutting and serving. Garnish each serving with lots of chopped fresh parsley.

You may make this dish a day ahead of time and rewarm before garnishing and serving.

Stroganoff Seitansky

6 SERVINGS

SERVING SUGGESTION

Start with a California Caesar salad (page 169), and end with any dessert pleaser.

¼ cup olive or sunflower oil

1½ lbs seitan, cut into ½-inch cubes

6 shallots, peeled and sliced

1 cup sliced mushrooms

2 Tbsp unbleached flour

3 cups soy milk

½ cup white wine

1 Tbsp Dijon mustard

½ tsp black pepper

1 lb cooked pasta, such as linguine, tagliatelle, or fettuccine

¼ cup chopped fresh parsley

....

Heat olive oil in a saucepan and sauté seitan and shallots until shallots are transparent and lightly browned. Add mushrooms for 1 minute, then sprinkle in flour and sauté another minute. Mix in soy milk and wine, mustard, salt, and pepper, and simmer until thickened. Portion pasta on plates and top with Stroganoff. Garnish with chopped parsley.

Seitan Olé Molé

6 SERVINGS

SERVING SUGGESTION

Serve with warmed corn tortillas, Mama's Mexican Rice (page 256), and José y Jesus' Jicama Salad (page 173). ¡Olé!

½ cup chopped raw almonds

½ cup pumpkin seeds

¼ cup sesame seeds

¼ cup unsweetened cocoa powder

3 Tbsp chili powder

1 tsp ground coriander

½ tsp cinnamon

¼ cup olive or sunflower oil

4 garlic cloves, chopped

½ cup finely chopped onion

1½ Tbsp sea salt

2 medium tomatoes, chopped

2 cups water

¼ cup cider vinegar

1 cup raisins

1½ lbs seitan, cut into ½-inch cubes

Garnish

1½ cups loosely packed fresh cilantro leaves

½ cup toasted sesame seeds

½ cup raisins

Grind chopped almonds, pumpkin seeds, and sesame seeds in a blender or suribachi. In a small skillet on medium heat, roast the nut-and-seed mixture along with the cocoa powder, chili powder, coriander, and cinnamon. Keep stirring. When the aroma begins to arise and the mixture is lightly toasted, set aside. Keep stirring when you first remove the pan from the heat, as the mixture could still burn on the bottom of the hot pan.

In another skillet, heat olive oil and sauté onion and garlic until transparent and lightly browned. Purée cooked onion-garlic mixture in blender along with nuts-and-seeds mixture, salt, tomatoes, water, vinegar, and raisins. Transfer purée to a large saucepan; add cubed seitan and let simmer, uncovered, stirring occasionally, 20–30 minutes. Portion in bowls, and top with garnish of cilantro leaves, sesame seeds, and raisins.

BUY FREE TRADE COCOA

As this is written, more information is being published about the slavery of young boys working on cocoa plantations in West Africa. Please buy Free Trade cocoa if possible, or at least steer away from cocoa of West African origins until the cocoa cartels make some policy changes. See www.earthsave.org for more information on this and other earth issues.

Tofu Short Stack

4 SERVINGS

This dish walks tall.

1 lb firm Chinese-style tofu, drained and cut into 8 slices

2 cups cooked quinoa (see table on page 62)

1 bunch fresh spinach, steamed

1 recipe Tequila Lime Yams (page 262)

1 cup cooked adzuki beans, drained

½ cup Mango Lime Vinaigrette (page 107)

• •

Preheat oven to 375°F. Marinate tofu slices in Basic Tofu Marinade, using the lemon and garlic variations (page 80), in a baking dish for 20–30 minutes. Bake tofu with marinade for 20 minutes.

For each serving, place about ¼ cup of quinoa in the center of a plate. Top with a slice of baked tofu, a spoonful of yams, then steamed spinach. Top spinach with another slice of tofu, off set at a 30° angle (for a kind of pinwheel appearance), then more yam and spinach. Drizzle Mango Lime Vinaigrette on top of each stack. Toss adzuki beans on top and around the plate for bonus nutrition and attractive effect.

Le Benedict Florentine

4 SERVINGS

VARIATION

Substitute steamed asparagus spears for spinach.

1 lb soft or medium Chinese-style tofu, drained and cut into 8 slices

1 bunch fresh spinach, steamed

1 cup Hollandaise Sauce (page 133)

8 slices vegetarian ham or bacon (Yves brand Canadian Veggie Bacon is a good choice)

four 3-inch squares of focaccia bread, sliced in half

8 slices tomato

1 tsp + 2 Tbsp Roasted Garlic Oil (see page 86) or nondairy margarine

3 Tbsp chopped fresh parsley for garnish

• •

Preheat oven to 375°F. Marinate tofu in Basic Tofu Marinade, using the lemon and garlic variations (page 80), in a baking dish for 20–30 minutes. Bake tofu with marinade for 20 minutes.

Meantime, prepare Hollandaise Sauce as described on page 133.

Heat the 1 teaspoon of Roasted Garlic Oil in a skillet and lightly sauté vegetarian ham or bacon slices on each side.

Toast focaccia bread, and lightly brush slices with Roasted Garlic Oil or spread with margarine. Place two slices of focaccia on a plate and top with sautéed vegetarian ham or bacon slice, a baked tofu slice, and steamed spinach. Then top with Hollandaise Sauce, and finally a tomato slice. Garnish with chopped parsley.

Fun Mung Curry

4–6 SERVINGS

1 cup mung beans

2 Tbsp olive or sunflower oil

1 tsp toasted sesame oil

1 onion, chopped

4 garlic cloves, sliced

1 tsp garam masala

$\frac{1}{2}$ tsp ground coriander

$\frac{1}{2}$ tsp turmeric

6 cups water

1 cup cubed yam ($\frac{1}{2}$-inch cubes)

$\frac{1}{2}$-inch slice fresh ginger root

1 medium zucchini or yellow squash, sliced into half moons

$1\frac{1}{2}$ cups cauliflower, cut or broken into small florets

1 Tbsp sea salt

1 Tbsp lemon juice

Garnish

$\frac{1}{2}$ cup chopped cilantro leaves

$\frac{1}{2}$ cup raisins or dried cranberries

$\frac{1}{2}$ cup roasted pumpkin seeds

Sort through the mung beans to look for bits of tiny stones and broken beans. (It's better to take a minute here and re-move these than wait until your dinner guests find a piece of something with their tooth!) Place beans in a colander or sieve; rinse under cool, clear water; and drain. It is not necessary to soak the beans, owing to the long cooking time. In a large saucepan, sauté onion and garlic in the oils until onion is transparent and lightly browned. Add garam masala, coriander, and turmeric, and sauté for 15 seconds. Add mung beans, water, yam, and ginger. Simmer, partially covered, for 45 minutes. Add zucchini or yellow squash, cauliflower, and salt. Simmer another 10–15 minutes. Remove from heat and stir in lemon juice. Garnish with cilantro, raisins, and toasted pumpkin seeds. Serve with basmati rice and Banana Coconut Chutney.

Banana Coconut Chutney

1 CUP

    1 medium banana

    1 cup loosely packed fresh cilantro

    ¾ cup unsweetened canned coconut milk

    ¼ cup fresh lime juice

    ¼ cup unsweetened shredded coconut

    1 tsp maple syrup

    ¾ tsp sea salt

Blend all ingredients together in a blender. Enjoy in splendor.

Mad Cowboy

SERVES 2 AND A PURPOSE

Many years ago, pre–Native Foods, I met a man named Howard Lyman. What he had to say inspired me, but more than anything his volition completely enraptured me.

Howard was a fifth-generation Montana cattle rancher, and a typical good cowboy. He used dioxin to kill flies, sprayed it everywhere. He used antibiotics and hormones to keep the dairy cows pumping, and separated many a baby cow from its mama in order to give American kids the cheese pizza slice of their life. After a tumor on his spine, and witnessing the premature deaths of family members and loved ones living the same lifestyle, he believed he saw the oxymoron of it all. The slice was their life.

Howard realized his business and lifestyle were not going in a direction that would help the environment and give nourishment and health to future generations. He had been raised in a generation that believed the farmer's role was to feed and support the people, but he saw how big business used that venue to create queen-sized revenue for themselves by using the small farmer as the worker bee. He felt that the right thing to do was walk away and then began a grass roots campaign and single-handedly scoured the country telling folks what he believed to be the truth. Fear of change stops people from doing many things in life, but Howard embraced it; for that he enraptured me.

With a pop star travel schedule, Howard tours the globe on his mission. I am inspired by people who "walk their talk"; it keeps me motivated. I sometimes refer to him as the Gandhi of the twenty-first century! This dish was named in honor of the maddest cowboy of 'em all, Howard Lyman.

3–4 soy brests, prepared according to Reconstitution for Soy Brests (page 76)

½ cup Bessie's (Thank-You) BBQ Sauce (page 128)

2 medium potatoes, baked

3–4 cups steamed mixed veggies of your choice

4 Tbsp Black Creek Ranch Dressing (page 113)

¼ cup chopped green onions

¼ cup fresh or defrosted frozen corn kernels

1 Tbsp Brunoise-cut red bell pepper (see page 45)

Preheat oven to 350°F. Slice each brest into three slices lengthwise. Skewer the slices on four bamboo skewers. Slather BBQ sauce on brests, reserving extra sauce for garnish. Place on a cookie sheet or baking dish, and bake for 20 minutes.

Cut each baked potato in half and put in a bowl or on a plate. Top with 1 tablespoon of Black Creek Ranch Dressing. Mound steamed veggies on top and add another tablespoon of dressing. Stick the two skewers into the potatoes or place them on top. Drizzle the remaining BBQ sauce on top. Garnish with green onions, corn, and chopped red bell pepper.

Eggplant Rollatini

6 SERVINGS

2 large eggplants, sliced lengthwise into ¼-inch slices

½ tsp sea salt

3 sautéed tempeh patties (see page 65), each 2½ –3 oz

⅓ cup sunflower or safflower oil

2 cups Tofu Ricotta (page 98)

3 cups Simple Marinara (page 118)

18 steamed broccoli florets

2–3 Tbsp Pumpkin Seed Pesto (page 123)

6 large basil leaves

2 Tbsp Brunoise-cut red bell pepper (see page 45)

....

Preheat oven to 375°F. Arrange eggplant slices on a baking tray. "Sweat" eggplant by sprinkling with salt and waiting 10 minutes as water escapes. This helps to remove bitterness. Wipe water ("sweat") from eggplant with paper towels.

Chop tempeh into ½-inch cubes.

Heat 3 tablespoons of the oil in a skillet until hot. Add eggplant slices and sauté until softened and browned.

On each sautéed eggplant slice, place a heaping table-spoon of Tofu Ricotta and 4–5 cubes tempeh on one end. Roll eggplant around the filling. Place stuffed eggplant rolls in a baking dish, and top with 2 cups of marinara. Cover with lid or foil and bake for 30 minutes.

Arrange rolls atop rice on plates and top with some extra marinara sauce. Arrange 3 broccoli florets around the perimeter of each plate. Garnish with Pumpkin Seed Pesto, fresh basil leaves, and chopped red bell pepper.

Chicken Fried Steak

4–6 SERVINGS

SERVING SUGGESTION

Serve with Roasted Garlic Mashed Potatoes (page 258), Shallot Mushroom Gravy (page 125), and Get Yo' Greens (page 259).

VARIATION

Use ¼- inch-thick slices of seitan instead of soy brests.

1 cup coconut milk

½ cup water

4 garlic cloves, chopped

1½ tsp sea salt

1½ tsp dried thyme

6 soy brests, prepared according to Reconstitution for Soy Brests (page 76)

2 cups unbleached flour

½ cup sunflower or safflower oil

··

In a bowl, combine coconut milk, water, garlic, salt, and thyme. Dip soy brests in coconut milk mixture, then dredge in flour mixture. Repeat so that brests get coated in a nice amount of batter. Heat oil in a skillet. Make sure oil is hot, and cook brests until golden brown.

Flaming Fajitas

4–6 SERVINGS

2–3 Tbsp olive or sunflower oil

1 red bell pepper, sliced lengthwise

½ green bell pepper, sliced lengthwise

½ yellow bell pepper, sliced lengthwise

1 tsp cumin seed

½ tsp sea salt

¼ tsp black pepper

¼ tsp crushed red chilies

1 lb seitan, thinly sliced

1 dozen corn tortillas, warmed

2 cups Salsa Fresca (page 121)

1 avocado, sliced

Heat olive oil in a skillet and sauté onion until transparent and lightly browned. Add bell peppers and sauté for another 2 minutes. Add cumin seed, salt, pepper, and crushed red chilies. Toss in thinly sliced seitan strips. Stir-fry for another minute until flavors blend. Assemble by filling warm corn tortillas with sautéed seitan mixture, then topping with salsa and sliced avocado. Ingredients can be served separately, and guests can assemble them individually.

Steak Morocco

4 SERVINGS

1 lb seitan, cut into ½-inch slices (If seitan is store-bought, slices will probably be smaller.)

1 cup Rockin' Moroccan Marinade (page 132)

4 Tbsp Toasted Almond and Currant Chutney (page 88)

2 Tbsp chopped fresh parsley

···

Preheat oven to 425°F. Place seitan slices in a baking dish and pour marinade over them. Marinate 20–30 minutes. Drain excess marinade. Bake for 10–12 minutes. Place 1 tablespoon Toasted Almond and Currant Chutney on top of each serving. Garnish with chopped parsley.

SERVING SUGGESTION

Serve with quinoa and Roasted Winter Roots and Vegetables (page 248).

VARIATION

Instead of baking, cook seitan on indoor or outdoor grill.

Thai Tempeh Stir-Fry

4 SERVINGS

VARIATION

Substitute firm Chinese-style tofu for tempeh.

¼ cup soy sauce

¼ cup fresh lime juice

¼ cup maple syrup

1 tsp grated fresh ginger

2 garlic cloves, minced

¼ tsp crushed red chilies

¼ cup olive or sunflower oil

½ lb tempeh, cut into ½-inch cubes

½ red bell pepper, cut into ½-inch squares

1 cup chopped green onions

1 cup bean sprouts

1 cup julienne-cut snow peas

1½ cups shredded green cabbage

1 cup loosely packed cilantro leaves

½ cup roasted and ground peanuts

¼ cup toasted shredded coconut

In small bowl, combine soy sauce, lime juice, maple syrup, ginger, garlic, and chilies. Heat oil in skillet and sauté tempeh cubes until golden brown. Add bell peppers and sauté another 1–2 minutes. Pour soy sauce mixture over and stir-fry until liquid is reduced to half. Add green onions, bean sprouts, snow peas, and cabbage, and toss well. Arrange on a serving platter or in individual bowls. Garnish with cilantro, peanuts, and coconut.

Good Karma Sarma: Cabbage Rolls

6–8 SERVINGS

If this recipe makes more than you need, make it anyway and keep the extra rolls for a quick lunch or freeze for later. This is one of those "make ahead" dishes that gets better the next day.

2 large green cabbages

⅓ cup olive oil or sunflower oil

2 onions, finely chopped

1 cup reconstituted textured soy protein granules, bits, or flakes (see page 74)

½ cup uncooked brown rice

½ cup uncooked jasmine rice

28-oz can crushed peeled tomatoes

1 cup canned or bottled sauerkraut, drained

½ cup water

1 cup chopped parsley

½ cup chopped mint

2 tsp sea salt

½ tsp black pepper

lemon slices and chopped parsley for garnish

. . . .

Remove the core from the bottom of each cabbage and place both in a large pot with 2 inches of water. (If your pot isn't large enough for both cabbages, steam one at a time.) Cover and steam for 25 minutes.

In a skillet, sauté onions in oil until transparent and lightly browned. Add soy protein and raw brown and jasmine rice, and sauté 2–3 minutes. Add tomatoes, sauerkraut, water, parsley, mint, salt, and pepper. Stir well, cover, and simmer 15 minutes.

Preheat oven to 375°F. After cabbage has steamed and cooled, separate leaves. Place each leaf, seam side up, on a work table or cutting board. Put a large spoonful of the soy protein–rice mixture in the center of each leaf; fold in the sides of the leaf, and then roll.

Arrange stuffed leaves in a lightly oiled baking dish. When the dish is full, add 1 inch of water and cover with a lid or foil. Bake for 1½ hours. Let cool 10 minutes before serving. Garnish with chopped parsley and lemon slices.

SERVING SUGGESTION

Garnish each serving with a dollop of soy sour cream.

VARIATION

You can omit either the sauerkraut or the textured soy protein.

The Hollywood Bowl

2 SERVINGS

Honor the celebrity within
yourself and enjoy a favorite
of the Hollywood set.

½ lb firm Chinese-style tofu, sliced and marinated
   (see Basic Tofu Marinade, page 80)

4 cups steamed mixed veggies

½ cup Thai Peanut Sauce (page 122)

3 cups cooked brown rice

½ cup chopped green onions

2 Tbsp roasted peanuts

1 Tbsp Brunoise-cut red bell pepper (see page 45)

Slice tofu on the diagonal for an attractive appearance, and
marinate 20–30 minutes in Basic Tofu Marinade.

Steam a variety of vegetables (such as broccoli, carrots,
cauliflower, zucchini, and kale), with marinated tofu on top
of veggies to steam along with them. When vegetables are
done, carefully remove the tofu and set aside. Portion rice
into two bowls, then top with veggies. Portion Thai Peanut
Sauce over veggies, then top with the tofu. Garnish with
green onions, roasted peanuts, and chopped red bell pepper.

Sweet and Sour Nuggets

4 SERVINGS

These vegetarian nuggets make a good transition for kids getting off the "other" kind. It's also a good way to get them to eat their veggies. Offer children other sauces they may like to dip the nuggets and veggies in. Adults fare well with this advice too!

1 cup unbleached flour

1 tsp baking powder

½ tsp sea salt

1½ cups unflavored soda water

½ cup sunflower or safflower oil

1 cup reconstituted textured soy protein chunks (see page 74)

6 cups cooked jasmine rice

2 cups Sassy Sweet and Sour Sauce (page 126)

2 cups julienne-cut snow peas

2 cups julienne-cut carrots

1 cup chopped green onions

¼ cup toasted sesame seeds

¼ cup Brunoise-cut red bell pepper (see page 45)

....

In a bowl, mix together flour, baking powder, and sea salt. Whisk in soda water to form a thick batter. In a skillet, heat oil until very hot. Dip textured soy protein chunks in batter and then drop in hot oil until crispy. Do this in batches, so as to keep oil temperature steady. Leaving space around the chunks as they fry will prevent their sticking together and will ensure browning quickly and evenly.

Remove nuggets from pan and drain on paper towels on a plate. Portion rice in four bowls and top with crispy nuggets and Sassy Sweet and Sour Sauce. Garnish with snow peas, carrots, green onions, sesame seeds, and chopped red bell pepper.

Puff Pastry Pot Pies

6 SERVINGS

1 sheet frozen puff pastry

1 carrot, cut into ¼-inch cubes

½ cup chopped celery

1 cup edamame (shelled green soybeans)

2 medium potatoes, cut into ½-inch cubes

3 cups water

2½ tsp sea salt

⅓ cup olive or sunflower oil

1 onion, chopped

3 Tbsp unbleached flour

½ cup soy milk

1 lb seitan, cut into ½-inch cubes

4 Tbsp hemp seeds

....

Remove puff pastry from freezer and let it slightly defrost (about 20 minutes) so it's workable.

In a saucepan, put carrot, celery, edamame, potatoes, water, and salt, and bring to a boil. Reduce heat and simmer 10 minutes, or until potatoes are soft.

Heat oil in another saucepan, and sauté onion until transparent and lightly browned. Sprinkle with 3 tablespoons flour, and stir until flour is lightly browned and mixture is thickened. Add soy milk and stir to blend; then add seitan, hemp seeds, and simmered veggie mixure. Heat until thickened. Preheat oven to 400°F. Lightly roll out puff pastry sheet on a lightly floured surface. Cut into six rounds the size of the bowl you are serving in. (If your bowls are larger, you may need to use a second sheet of puff pastry.) Bake on an ungreased cookie sheet for about 15 minutes, until puffed and golden brown. Portion warmed seitan-veggie mixture into serving bowls, and top each with a puff pastry round.

VARIATIONS

• *Use ovenproof bowls, place uncooked puff pastry rounds on top, and bake the bowls until top is puffed and golden brown. These will stay warm for a long time. Caution guests about the heat if serving immediately.*
• *Substitute reconstituted textured soy protein chunks (page 75) or firm Chinese-style tofu for seitan.*

Pasta Bolognese

4 SERVINGS

Pasta Bolognese is good for spontaneously thinking of four good friends to invite over Friday night and then surprising them with dinner … and maybe a little song.

Bolognese (bo-luh-NEEZ) refers to the cooking style of Bologna, Italy. Someone there decided to add ground meat to marinara sauce, and the name stuck. What didn't stick is the kind of meat they used; this version uses soy meat—yeah!

1 lb cooked pasta (linguine or spaghetti works well)
1 cup Italian Ground Around (page 75)
2 cups Simple Marinara (page 118)
4 Tbsp Pumpkin Seed Pesto (page 123)
¼ cup chopped fresh parsley

• •

Portion pasta in bowls and top with hot Italian Ground Around and Simple Marinara. Garnish with Pumpkin Seed Pesto and chopped fresh parsley.

SERVING SUGGESTIONS

• *Garnish plate with some steamed broccoli and carrots.*
• *Serve with green salad with Basic Balsamic Vinaigrette (page 104) and Garlic Toast (page 87).*

Rasta Pasta Primavera

6 SERVINGS

1 lb seitan, cut into ½-inch cubes
¾ cup Jamaican Jerk Marinade (page 130)
1 lb cooked pasta (rigatoni or penne works well)
4 cups steamed mixed veggies
2 cups Simple Marina (page 118)
6 Tbsp Pumpkin Seed Pesto (page 123)
18–20 Roasted Garlic Cloves (page 86)
¼ cup chopped fresh parsley
6 large basil leaves

In a skillet, heat seitan cubes with Jerk Marinade until most of the marinade has been reduced. Portion pasta in six serving bowls or plates, and top with steamed veggies, marinara, and seitan cubes. Garnish each bowl with 1 tablespoon Pumpkin Seed Pesto, 3–4 Roasted Garlic Cloves, and a basil leaf.

Jerked "Save the Chicken"

4 SERVINGS

4–6 reconstituted soy brests (see page 76)
1½ cups Jamaican Jerk Marinade (page 130)
¼ cup olive, safflower, or sunflower oil

....

In a bowl or baking dish, cover soy brests with marinade and marinate 1 hour. Drain excess marinade from brests. Heat oil in skillet, and sauté to brown on both sides. You may also brush with oil and grill.

VARIATIONS

• *Instead of soy brests, use seitan or firm Chinese-style tofu.*
• *Brush marinated brests, seitan, or tofu with oil, and bake on oiled cookie sheet at 375° for 20–25 minutes.*

SERVING SUGGESTION

Serve with Coconut Groove Rice (page 253) and baked yams. Drizzle excess marinade on rice and/or yams.

side dishes

*T*his chapter presents vegetables, breakfast dishes, and other good things.

Kissed French Toast

This recipe was adapted from the Brothers of Holy Protection Orthodox Monastery. I recommend their book, *Simply Heavenly: The Monastery Vegetarian Cookbook,* by their abbot, George Burke—it's completely vegan.

1½ cups water

3 Tbsp soy flour or unbleached pastry flour

2 Tbsp melted nondairy margarine

1 Tbsp kuzu or cornstarch

1 Tbsp maple syrup

¼ tsp almond extract

¼ tsp cinnamon

¼ tsp turmeric

pinch sea salt

2–3 Tbsp organic shortening

six 1-inch slices French bread or sourdough

pure maple syrup for serving

Blend all ingredients, except last three, in a blender. Place mixture in a saucepan, and whisk while heating until mixture is thickened. Remove from heat and slightly cool.

Melt some shortening in a skillet (cast iron works well for this) while soaking bread in batter. Place bread in skillet and brown on each side. Let it get nice and brown before turning, as the batter is sticky. Use a spatula and scrape the bottom of the pan well while turning.

Serve with pure maple syrup, and see you in heaven!

Tofu Scrambler

4–6 SERVINGS

½ cup chopped onion

½ red bell pepper, chopped

2 Tbsp olive or sunflower oil

1 lb medium or firm Chinese-style (not silken) tofu

¼ tsp sea salt

¼ tsp black pepper

¼ tsp turmeric

1 cup chopped green onions

....

Heat oil in a skillet and sauté onions and bell pepper until onions are transparent and lightly browned. Crumble in tofu, and add salt, pepper, and turmeric. Sauté another 2–3 minutes. Garnish with chopped green onions.

VARIATIONS

• *Add chopped seitan when sautéing onions or chopped vegetarian sausage links.*
• *Substitute curry powder for turmeric.*

SERVING SUGGESTION

Let Scrambler cool and add 2 tablespoons vegan mayonnaise and ¼ cup chopped celery, and call it Tofu Egg Salad!

In Thyme for Breakfast Potatoes

6 SERVINGS

4 medium-sized potatoes

⅓ cup olive or sunflower oil

1 onion, chopped

1 tsp sea salt

¼ tsp black pepper

½ tsp dried thyme

1 cup chopped green onions

• •

Slice potatoes in half lengthwise, and then cut each half in ¼-inch half-moon slices. Heat oil in skillet and sauté onions for 2 minutes. Place potato slices on top of onions and cook on medium to low heat, partially covered, for 10–12 minutes. Add salt, pepper, and thyme, and stir mixture so as to slightly brown both sides of potatoes. Partially cover and cook another 10 minutes. Remove cover, and stir to brown and cook until potatoes are soft. Remove from heat and stir in green onions.

VARIATION

Use leftover baked or boiled potatoes, and reduce the cooking time.

Cranberry Chestnut Stuffing

APPROX. 8 CUPS:
ENOUGH TO STUFF
4–6 ADULT MOUTHS

1 cup minced shallots

½ cup olive oil

6 cups slightly stale bread cut into ½-inch cubes

2 cups chopped cooked peeled chestnuts

1 cup dried cranberries

1 cup fresh chopped parsley

1½ tsp sea salt

¼ tsp white pepper

⅔ cup soy milk

Preheat oven to 350°F. Heat olive oil in a skillet, and sauté shallots until transparent and lightly browned. Add cubed bread, chestnuts, cranberries, parsley, salt, and pepper, and sauté 2–3 minutes, combining well. Add soy milk and sauté another 2 minutes. Place in an oiled 9 x 13–inch baking dish and bake, uncovered, for 20 minutes.

SERVING SUGGESTIONS

• *Use as a filling for baked winter squash.*
• *Serve with Tempeh Scaloppine with Shallot Mushroom Gravy (page 125) and Cranberry Orange Relish (page 93) to save a turkey's life for Thanksgiving.*

Roasted Winter Roots and Vegetables

6–8 SERVINGS

I like to add the different vegetables not only for their flavors but because it leads to conversation about what kind they are. Always have to be educating! You can add other veggies and leave out what isn't available.

SERVING SUGGESTION

If you're serving less than the recipe calls for, you can always use the leftovers as a salad the next day; just toss with a little Basic Balsamic Vinaigrette (page 104), Green Goddess (page 105), or Madison's Garden Dressing (page 115).

2 medium yams or sweet potatoes, cut into 1-inch cubes

½ lb brussel sprouts, cut into halves

3 medium carrots, cut into ½-inch slices

2 medium parsnips, cut into ¼-inch slices

2 Yukon gold potatoes, cut into 1-inch cubes

1 turnip, cut into 1-inch cubes

2 medium red onions, quartered

2 cups (approx. 1 lb) peeled chestnuts

3- to 4-inch piece lotus root, cut into ¼-inch slices

1 cup dried cranberries or dried sweet cherries

½ cup olive oil

2 tsp sea salt

2 tsp chopped fresh rosemary

½ cup water

Preheat oven to 400°F. In a large bowl, toss vegetables with olive oil, salt, and rosemary. Transfer to a roasting pan and drizzle water evenly over vegetables. Bake until tender, 35–40 minutes, stirring every 10 minutes or so to cook evenly.

Sautéed Chard with Onions

4–6 SERVINGS

This is one of my favorite vegetable dishes. Something about that combination of earthy chard flavor and onion sweetness makes me sing.

1 bunch red chard
2 medium yellow onions, sliced
2–3 Tbsp olive oil
½ tsp sea salt

....

Cut about 1 inch off the ends of the chard stems and discard. Separate stems from leaves. Cut stems into 1-inch pieces, and cut leaves into 1-inch strips.

In a large skillet, sauté onion until transparent. Add chard stems and sauté for 2 minutes. Put chard leaves on top of stems in skillet and wait about 1 minute before mixing. This gives them a chance to wilt a bit, making them easier to mix in, and the onions have a chance to brown a little more. Salt gently while sautéing until tender.

VARIATION

Instead of chard, use beet greens—another one of my absolute favorites. (You can use the beets for the Perestroika salad, page 177.)

Tzimmes

4 SERVINGS

Vegan Jewish New Year has arrived. The Rosh Hashanah holiday is a time for sweet dishes such as tzimmes.

⅓ cup olive oil

1 onion, finely chopped

1½ lbs seitan, cut into 1-inch cubes

4 cups water

2 medium sweet potatoes, sliced in half lengthwise and cut into ½-inch half-moon slices

1 cup pitted prunes

⅓ cup maple syrup

1 tsp salt

¼ tsp pepper

¼ tsp cinnamon

2 Tbsp kuzu

⅓ cup cold water

Heat oil in a soup pot and sauté onions until transparent. Add seitan cubes and sauté until nicely browned. Add rest of ingredients except kuzu and ⅓ cup water. Simmer, partially covered, for 30–40 minutes. Dissolve kuzu in ⅓ cup cold water and add to soup pot. Stir until thickened. Mixture should be thick and not soupy.

Have a sweet New Year!

Steamed Artichokes

4 SERVINGS

In my opinion, no one eats enough artichokes. Many people tell me they don't know how to cook or how to eat them. Here's the secret that's OK to share with everyone!

SERVING SUGGESTION

Dip leaves and heart in Caesar's Vegan dressing (page 112), Black Creek Ranch Dressing (page 113), or Hollandaise Sauce (page 133). Vegan mayonnaise mixed with a little lemon juice is also popular.

2 lemons

8 cups water

1 tsp sea salt

4 medium-large artichokes

• •

Trim rind from lemons with a peeler. Put water in a large pot, and add lemon rind and salt. Cut rindless lemons in half. Cut off the stem of each artichoke and rub it with the open end of a lemon to release the lemon juice. This keeps the cut stem from turning dark.

Using a sharp knife, cut about 1½ inches off of top of each artichoke and rub with lemon. With kitchen scissors, trim about ½ inch off of each leaf to remove the prickly point, and rub the leaf tips all over with lemon.

Bring your potful of water, lemon rind, and salt to a boil. Separate artichoke leaves slightly, then place top down in boiling water. Keep on a low boil and cook, partially covered, for 40 minutes. To test doneness, insert a fork into the center of the artichoke stem; it should pierce it easily. Remove artichokes from water and cool slightly.

HOW TO EAT ARTICHOKES

Pull off a leaf and, holding the trimmed end, turn it so that the outside of the leaf is facing up. Place it in your mouth, still holding trimmed end. Close your mouth over the leaf so that the little fleshy nub is behind your bottom front teeth. Pull the leaf out of your mouth, holding top and bottom teeth slightly separated, while scraping soft flesh and flesh from nub with your bottom teeth. That's it!

When you get to the center spiny translucent leaves with no flesh, gather with you fingertips and discard. It pulls out like a cone. Now you see the hairy choke. Using a teaspoon remove it. Now you are left with the heart. The absolute joy of the whole process is eating this part.

I like to squeeze a little lemon juice and sprinkle a pinch of sea salt and eat with my eyes closed.

Coconut Groove Rice

4–6 SERVINGS

2 cups water

1 cup coconut milk

¼ tsp sea salt

1 cup uncooked jasmine rice

½-inch piece fresh ginger, peeled and sliced

½ cup toasted shredded dried coconut (unsweetened)

½ cup chopped pineapple (fresh if possible)

2 Tbsp chopped cilantro

....

In a saucepan, bring water, coconut milk, and salt to a boil. Stir in rice and ginger. Cover and reduce heat to low, and cook 20 minutes, until liquid is absorbed. Remove ginger and let rice sit 5–10 minutes before transferring to bowl. Toss rice with coconut, pineapple, and cilantro.

VARIATION

Add ½ cup cashew pieces.

SERVING SUGGESTION

Great with Jerked "Save the Chicken" (page 242) and baked yams.

Vera's Voluptuous Veggie Fried Rice

4 SERVINGS

2 Tbsp olive or sunflower oil

1 tsp toasted sesame oil

⅓ cup diced carrot

⅓ cup diced red bell pepper

3 cups cooked, cooled rice of choice

½ cup diced seitan

⅓ cup fresh or frozen green peas

½ cup chopped green onions

1 tsp sea salt

2 Tbsp toasted sesame seeds

Heat oils in a skillet and sauté carrot and bell pepper for 1 minute. Add rice and stir-fry 1 minute, then add rest of ingredients and stir-fry for another minute or two. Garnish with sesame seeds.

Japanese Fried Rice

2 tsp olive or sunflower oil

1 tsp toasted sesame oil

1½ tsp grated fresh ginger

3 cups cooked short grain brown rice, cooled

½ cup cooked adzuki beans

⅓ cup edamame (shelled green soybeans)

1 tsp sugar (optional)

½ tsp sea salt

¼ cup chopped green onions

• •

Heat oils in a skillet and sauté ginger for 5 seconds. Add rest of ingredients and stir-fry another 1–2 minutes, until warmed through. Garnish with chopped green onions.

VARIATION

Use jasmine rice for a nice color contrast with the adzukis and soybeans.

Mama's Mexican Rice

4 SERVINGS

2 Tbsp olive or sunflower oil

1 onion, finely chopped

½ red bell pepper, finely chopped

½ cup uncooked jasmine rice

¼ tsp chili powder

2 cups canned peeled crushed or chopped tomatoes

½ cup water

2 bay leaves

½ tsp sea salt

⅛ tsp black pepper

· ·

Heat oil in a saucepan and sauté onion until transparent. Add red bell pepper and sauté another 2–3 minutes. Stir in rice and chili powder, and sauté until rice browns slightly. Add remaining ingredients, cover, and simmer 20 minutes. Uncover and simmer another 5 minutes to remove excess moisture. Remove bay leaves before serving.

SERVING SUGGESTION

Garnish with chopped black olives for a Betty Crocker '50s touch.

Love Potion Green Beans

4 SERVINGS

2 Tbsp olive oil

1 large Portobello mushroom, chopped

3 garlic cloves, sliced

½ tsp sea salt

1 lb green beans, trimmed and blanched

¼ tsp black pepper

Heat olive oil in a skillet and sauté mushroom with 2 pinches of the salt for 1 minute. Add garlic and sauté until mushrooms are golden brown, 2 minutes. Add green beans, remaining salt, and pepper. Toss until warmed through.

VARIATION

Instead of using fresh garlic cloves, use some sweet purée of Roasted Garlic Cloves (see page 86) when adding green beans.

Roasted Garlic Mashed Potatoes

4–6 SERVINGS

6 medium Yukon gold potatoes

2 cups water

1 tsp sea salt

½ cup soy milk

⅓ cup coconut milk

¼ cup Roasted Garlic Oil (see page 86)

10 Roasted Garlic Cloves (page 86)

sea salt and pepper to taste

Place potatoes in a large soup pot with water and salt, and bring to boil. Cover and lightly boil for 25–30 minutes. Let cool enough to remove skins. Place cooked potatoes in a bowl and add the rest of the ingredients with a mixer or by hand with a potato masher until incorporated.

Get Yo' Greens

4 SERVINGS

I hope this simple recipe inspires you to eat greens regularly. If not every day, try for three times a week—promise me.

SERVING SUGGESTIONS
• *Drizzle greens with Basic Balsamic Vinaigrette (page 104) or your favorite sauce or dressing.*
• *Serve with a grain and a favorite bean for a meal that's quick, nutritious, and easy to digest.*

1 bunch kale, collards, or chard

2–3 tsp lemon juice or umeboshi vinegar

2 tsp Gomasio (page 95)

Cut an inch off the bottom of greens stems and discard. Slice leaves and remaining stems into ½- to 1-inch strips and blanch. To blanch, bring approximately 4 cups of water to a boil with a pinch of sea salt. Add chard stems for 1 minute, then add leaves and cook about 2 minutes or until leaves are tender. (Reserve water and use to cook soups, grains, or beans.)

Sprinkle blanched greens with lemon juice or umeboshi vinegar and Gomasio.

KALE KICKS!

Kale has almost as much calcium as milk and also contains magnesium, which milk lacks. One cup of cooked kale is loaded with vitamins A and C, folic acid, potassium, and iron. It's no-fat and low-cal.

Roasted Lemon Potatoes

4–6 SERVINGS

6 medium potatoes (Yukon gold are good, but any will do)

½ cup olive oil

¼ cup lemon juice

1 tsp dried oregano

1½ tsp sea salt

....

Preheat oven to 425°F. Cut potatoes into wedges. Cover them with water in a bowl and drain to remove some starch. In a large bowl, toss potatoes with the rest of ingredients. Put them in a baking dish, and bake for 50 minutes, turning occasionally, until brown, crispy, and juicy.

Tangerine Yams

4 medium yams, boiled

2 Tbsp olive or sunflower oil

4 shallots, peeled and sliced

1½ cups fresh tangerine juice

¼ cup maple syrup

1 tsp sea salt

¼ tsp white pepper

Preheat oven to 375°F. Cool yams and remove skin, or leave on if you like. Cut yams into ½ inch rounds and arrange in a baking dish.

Heat oil in a saucepan, and sauté shallots until transparent and lightly browned. Add tangerine juice, maple syrup, salt, and white pepper. Simmer for 2–3 minutes. Pour over sliced yams and bake for 25 minutes.

VARIATION

If you can't find tangerine juice, substitute orange juice.

SERVING SUGGESTION

Top with Martha's Glazed Nuts (page 282) before serving.

Tequila Lime Yams

4 SERVINGS

2–3 Tbsp olive or sunflower oil

2 medium yams, grated (peeled first, if you wish)

½ tsp sea salt

2 Tbsp tequila

2 Tbsp lime juice

2 tsp maple syrup

½ cup dried cranberries (optional)

....

Heat oil in skillet and sauté grated yams for 2 minutes. Turn heat to medium-low and cook 10–15 minutes, partially covered, stirring occasionally. Add tequila, lime juice, maple syrup, and cranberries, and sauté another 5 minutes.

SERVING SUGGESTIONS

• *This recipe is used in the Tofu Short Stack (page 223).*
• *A nice accompaniment for sautéed tempeh or Jerked "Save the Chicken" (page 242).*

Leek 'n' Lemon

4–6 SERVINGS

I included this recipe because it's easy and really good, but also because I hope that people will eat more leeks. Many don't know what they are or what to do with them. Leeks are in the onion family; I think of them as giant green onions. They have a mild, sweet flavor.

2 medium leeks
1 lemon
2 tsp Gomasio (page 95)

∙∙

Remove the roots from the bulbs of the leeks if there are any. Cut older edges off the green leaves. Starting 2 inches from the bulb (root end), slice all the way through the stem to the leaves. Repeat 2 or 3 more times, creating strips but keeping the leek intact at root end. Wash well between the leaves to remove dirt. Cut leek into 2-inch pieces and blanch for about 4–5 minutes. Place in serving dish and squeeze the lemon over the top. Sprinkle with Gomasio.

VARIATION

Heat ¼ cup of olive oil in a skillet and place 2-inch pieces of leek in pan. Sprinkle with 1 teaspoon sea salt and let one side brown, then turn over and brown the other side. Slightly cover skillet until leeks are soft and tender.

Kasha Varnishkas

6 SERVINGS

A classic Jewish specialty of eastern Europe, this dish is traditionally made with eggs and chicken fat. Technically, varnishkas refers to the small bow-tie pasta usually used. My "save the chicken" version of the recipe uses large noodles and is baked, instead of cooked on the stovetop pilaf-style.

2 cups cooked buckwheat groats (see table on page 62)

½ lb fettuccine or other large flat noodle pasta, cooked according to package instructions

2 large onions, minced

¼ cup olive oil

½ tsp sea salt

1½ Tbsp poppy seeds

....

Preheat oven to 350°F. Heat oil in a skillet and sauté onion with salt until transparent and lightly browned. Add groats and pasta and mix well. Put into oiled baking dish and bake for 15 minutes.

Fred's Corn Bread

8 x 8–INCH BREAD

2 cups corn flour (see page 20)

2 cups unbleached flour

4 tsp baking powder

¼ tsp sea salt

1¼ cups water

¾ cup sunflower or safflower oil

¾ cup maple syrup

4 oz firm silken tofu (aseptic package)

1 orange, juiced and zested

½ tsp ground cardamom (optional)

....

Preheat oven to 375°F. In a mixing bowl, sift corn flour and unbleached flour, baking powder, and sea salt. Place the rest of the ingredients in a blender and mix well. Mix wet into dry ingredients. Place batter in an 8 x 8–inch baking pan or a 10-inch cast-iron skillet. Bake for 25–30 minutes. The top of the bread should crack nicely when done.

SERVING SUGGESTIONS

• *Great served for breakfast with jam.*

• *For a quick version of tamale pie, scoop black beans or pinto beans (or Neato Refritos, page 269) on top of a piece of Fred's Corn Bread (page 265). Top with veggies, salsa, and a dressing.*

East Indian Onion Bread (Naan)

16 PIECES

In Uzbekistan, this bread is called *non*. It's also a very popular bread in regions of China.

6 Tbsp olive or sunflower oil
1 large onion, finely chopped
¾ cup lukewarm water
1 tsp sea salt
2½–3 cups unbleached flour

···

Heat 2 tablespoons oil in a skillet and sauté onions until transparent. Let cool to room temperature. In a large mixing bowl, combine remaining oil and water, and stir in the onions and salt. Begin adding the flour ½ cup at a time until you get a dough that does not stick to your fingers. Gather the dough into a ball and then divide it into 16 pieces. With the palms of your hand, shape each piece into about a 2-inch ball. Roll out each ball into an 8-inch circle or 10-inch oblong. In the center of a hot, dry skillet (cast iron is good for this) place one rolled-out dough piece. Cook until brown, about 3–4 minutes on each side. Repeat with each piece of dough. Place in a basket or other porous vessel until serving.

If serving the next day or so, place bread on a cookie sheet and warm for 5–10 minutes at 300°F until firmed.

Won't You Arame, Bill

4 SERVINGS

Not only is diet about what
you eat, but it's about right
relationship in life as well.
That's what my macrobiotic
counselor friend, Mina
Dovic, discusses. Bill might
be thinking twice about mar-
riage, but never again will he
be afraid of arame after trying
this dish. Arame is a sea vegetable with a mild flavor and
lots of iron and calcium.
Makes Bill manly.

1 cup dried arame

1 onion, thinly sliced

½ tsp toasted sesame oil

¾ cup water

2 tsp soy sauce

••

Put arame in a bowl with water for a few minutes, then
rinse. Heat the sesame oil in a skillet and sauté onions 2
minutes. Spread onions evenly in pan and place arame on
top; then pour water over. Cover and simmer 20 minutes.
Add soy sauce and simmer, covered, another 5–10 minutes.

SERVING SUGGESTION

*Add a couple of spoonfuls as an accompaniment to whatever
you are eating. I like it with Leek 'n' Lemon (page 263) and
Japanese Fried Rice (page 255) for a quick-service dinner option.*

Hijiki à la Tanji

Hijiki is a dense sea veggie whose great black color and noodle-like appearance make it an attractive accompaniment to a meal.

This dish is named after the Tanjis, a wonderful Japanese-American family with whom I've eaten and traveled well.

½ cup dried hijiki
2 tsp olive or sunflower oil
1 tsp toasted sesame oil
1 carrot, cut julienne
1 Tbsp soy sauce
1 Tbsp rice vinegar
2 tsp maple syrup
½ cup edamame (shelled green soybeans)
1 Tbsp toasted sesame seeds

Rinse hijiki in a colander and then place it in a bowl and cover with water. Soak for 10 minutes, then drain.

Heat oils in a skillet and sauté carrot for 2–3 minutes. Add hijiki and sauté another 2–3 minutes. Add soy sauce, rice vinegar, and maple syrup, and simmer on low heat until liquid is absorbed and reduced. Add green soy beans, toss, and serve garnished with sesame seeds.

SERVING SUGGESTION

Serve ¼ cup as a starter before a meal, or as a snack at teatime when you want to dare to be different.

Neato Refritos: Mexican Refried Beans

4–6 SERVINGS

¼ cup olive oil

4 cups cooked pinto beans

1 tsp chopped garlic

½ cup cooking liquid from beans or water

sea salt to taste

Heat olive oil in a skillet and add about 1 cup of the beans and the garlic. Mash them, adding a little of the cooking liquid to help give good consistency. Continue adding beans with cooking liquid and stirring until all beans are mashed. Add salt to season.

VARIATIONS

Add ½ teaspoon chopped pepper, or 1 or 2 teaspoons Salsa de Chupacabra (page 100) with the garlic, to up the spice factor.

SERVING SUGGESTIONS

• *Use as a dip.*
• *Great in burritos.*
• *On a Sunday morning serve with Tofu Scrambler (page 245), Mama's Mexican Rice (page 256), Salsa Fresca (page 121), and warmed corn tortillas for a new take on huevos rancheros.*

Summer Grilled Vegetables

4–6 SERVINGS

VARIATIONS

Add some chopped fresh rosemary when tossing with olive oil.

SERVING SUGGESTIONS

• Serve with the Mad Cowboy (page 227) instead of steamed veggies.
• Drizzle with Pumpkin Seed Pesto (page 123) just before serving.
• Serve chilled the next day, drizzled with Basic Balsamic Vinaigrette (page 104) and fresh herbs such as basil, rosemary, or thyme. Madison's Garden Dressing (page 115) also is lovely with these, especially if the veggies are from a farmers' market.

1 zucchini

1 yellow squash

1 carrot

1 red onion

1 red bell pepper

1 large Portobello mushroom

¼ cup olive oil or Roasted Garlic Oil (page 86)

½ tsp sea salt

....

Cut zucchini and yellow squash into 1-inch pieces using the roll cut (see page 46).

Cut carrot into ¼-inch slices on a diagonal.

Peel red onion, and cut into eight quarter wedges.

Remove core and stem from red bell pepper, and cut into 1-inch strips.

Slice Portobello mushroom into ½-inch slices.

In a large bowl, toss all the vegetables except Portobello mushrooms with most of the oil and sea salt. Reserve about 1 tablespoon of oil and a couple of pinches of salt in a separate bowl for coating the mushroom slices so as not to break them up by tossing with the other vegetables.

Place vegetables on a hot grill, and cook so that they are lightly browned with grill marks and their moisture has begun to release, about 5 minutes per side. The squash may cook faster than the rest.

Serve warm.

sweet treats

While sugar and sweets are not recommended for daily eating, they are certainly here to stay for a while. We should probably try to steer away from eating them too often and replace that craving with something better like making love, but since that may not always be an option, here again Native Foods attempts to do what we do best and create some fun "alter-natives"!

These desserts are healthier options for your sweet tooth. There are a few macrobiotic-style choices without any added sugar as well.

Carrot Cake with Dream Cheese Frosting

9-INCH ROUND OR
8-INCH SQUARE CAKE

2 cups unbleached pastry flour

1 cup sugar

1½ Tbsp baking powder

2 tsp baking soda

1½ tsp cinnamon

½ tsp sea salt

½ cup orange juice concentrate

½ cup sunflower or safflower oil

4 oz firm silken tofu (about ⅓ aseptic package)

2 Tbsp vanilla extract

1½ cups grated carrots

1 recipe Dream Cheese Frosting (page 273)

Garnish

five ¼-inch diagonal slices fresh carrot

5 sprigs fresh parsley

Preheat oven to 325°F. Grease and flour a 9-inch round cake pan or an 8 x 8 x 2–inch square baking pan. Sift the dry ingredients together in a large bowl. In a blender, purée the orange juice, oil, tofu, and vanilla. Fold liquid ingredients gradually into dry ingredients. Fold in grated carrots.

Pour into greased and floured pan. Bake for 35–40 minutes. Let cool on wire rack. Loosen edges and then invert onto serving platter. Frost with Dream Cheese Frosting.

Cut triangle shapes out of carrot slices to resemble a miniature carrot and place on cake for garnish. Put a small sprig of parsley above the flat edge of the carrot garnish to resemble a carrottop. Oh so cute!

Dream Cheese Frosting

    8 oz soy cream cheese
    ⅓ cup maple syrup
    2 Tbsp orange zest (see page 48)
    1 orange, juiced
    2 tsp vanilla

. . . .

Place all ingredients in a bowl and whisk together until smooth.

Key Lime Parfait

6 SERVINGS

Share a parfait with a loved one and watch the mood go smooth, like the texture of this dessert.

KEY LIMES

The key lime is a small, round, juicy variety with a distinctive tartness. In California we call them Mexican limes. However, the larger, egg-shaped limes (known as Persian or Tahiti limes) work well in this recipe too.

2 cups granola (your favorite)

8 oz soy cream cheese

12 oz firm silken tofu (aseptic package)

½ cup soy milk

½ cup sugar

¼ cup fresh key lime juice (or regular lime juice)

zest of 1 lime (see page 48)

Grind granola in a blender until it has the consistency of coarse flour. Remove from blender and set aside. Rinse blender, and then put in soy cream cheese, tofu, soy milk, sugar, lime juice, and lime zest. Purée until smooth and well blended.

Place about 2 tablespoons of ground granola in the bottom of each of six 8-ounce parfait glasses or wineglasses. Pour cream cheese–tofu mixture over granola. Top with approximately another 2 tablespoons granola. Refrigerate at least 1 hour before serving.

SERVING SUGGESTION

• *Garnish with curls of fresh lime zest.*
• *Serve topped with fresh blueberries or peaches for a luscious brunch treat.*

Chai Pumpkin Pie

9-INCH PIE

2 cups (15-oz can) canned pumpkin

12.5 oz firm silken tofu (aseptic package)

1 cup maple syrup

2 Tbsp sunflower or safflower oil

3 Tbsp unbleached flour

1½ tsp ground cinnamon

1½ tsp ground cardamom

1 tsp fresh grated ginger

1 tsp vanilla extract

¼ tsp ground nutmeg

¼ tsp black pepper

1½ cups Vanilla Crème (page 301)

1 recipe Flaky Pie Crust, unbaked (page 277)

....

Preheat oven to 350°F. Place first eleven ingredients in a blender and blend well. Pour into unbaked Flaky Pie Crust and bake for 1 hour. Serve with Vanilla Crème (page 301).

VARIATION

Top with Martha's Glazed Nuts (page 282) before serving.

Mr. Weld's Banana Cream Pie

9-INCH PIE

My friend and mentor
Christopher Weld loved
dessert and was especially
fond of banana cream pie.
This recipe is dedicated to
Chris's memory, and may
his family continue to enjoy
this treat for generations to
come.

1½ cups (approx. 14 oz) canned coconut milk

1 box firm silken tofu (aseptic package)

1 cup sugar

3 tsp vanilla extract

¼ tsp sea salt

¼ cup kuzu or cornstarch, dissolved in ¼ cup cold water

4 bananas (2 mashed and 2 sliced)

½ cup toasted shredded unsweetened dried coconut (optional)

1 recipe Flaky Pie Crust, baked (page 277)

....

Purée coconut milk, tofu, sugar, vanilla, and salt in a blender. Heat mixture in a saucepan with kuzu dissolved in water while whisking constantly until thickened and bubbling. Remove from heat and stir in bananas. Pour into pre-baked Flaky Pie Crust and let set. Refrigerate at least 2 hours before serving. Top with toasted coconut before serving, if desired. (For toasting method, see page 48.)

Flaky Pie Crust

CRUST FOR A 9-INCH PIE

1½ cups unbleached flour

¼ tsp sea salt

½ cup chilled shortening

3–4 Tbsp ice water

Sift together flour and sea salt into a mixing bowl. Cut chilled shortening into flour mixture until it resembles a coarse meal. Add the ice water 1 tablespoon at a time, mixing in with a fork until the dough holds together. Form into a ball, wrap in plastic, and refrigerate 1 hour.

If you are prebaking the pie crust, preheat the oven to 425°F 10 minutes before the dough is ready. Roll out the dough onto a floured surface into a 12-inch round, then place in a 9-inch pie pan. Trim the edges, allowing for a ½-inch overhang, and then fold over and crimp. Prick the bottom and sides of the pastry with a fork.

To reduce shrinkage of the crust in the pie pan, place a sheet of waxed paper over the crust and fill with dried beans or rice. This will act as a weight. (Discard rice or beans after use or save for baking at a later date, as they will not be usable for cooking and eating.) Bake for 10–12 minutes.

Tastes Like Caramel Apple

This treat is fun for kids (and the young at heart) because when you eat the date and the apple slice at the same time, it tastes like a caramel apple!

1 apple, sliced in ½-inch slices

6 dates, pitted and sliced in half

....

Wrap a slice of date around an apple slice or lay it on top. However you do it, make sure you take a bite with both together.

Elephant Chocolate Cake

Did you know that most people love elephants and chocolate?

This recipe is dedicated to Carol Buckley and Tarra at the Elephant Sanctuary in Hohenwald, Tennessee.

1 cup unbleached flour

⅔ cup cocoa

2 Tbsp baking powder

2 tsp cinnamon

¾ cup sunflower or safflower oil

1 cup maple syrup

12.5 oz firm silken tofu (aseptic package)

1 tsp vanilla extract

¾ cup chocolate chips

Peanut Butter Cinnamon Topping (page 280)

....

Preheat oven to 350°F. Lightly grease and flour a 9-inch round cake pan. Sift dry ingredients into a bowl. Put oil, maple syrup, tofu, and vanilla in a blender, and blend well. Fold liquid ingredients into dry ingredients along with chocolate chips. Pour batter into the pan and bake for 25–30 minutes.

Let cake cool, then top with Peanut Butter Cinnamon Topping. You can also cut individual servings, then put a dollop of the topping on each serving. Sometimes I put the topping in a plastic squeeze bottle and make creative designs on each serving and on the plate.

Peanut Butter Cinnamon Topping

    1 cup smooth peanut butter

    1 tsp cinnamon

    ⅓ cup maple syrup

    ½ cup water

....

Purée all ingredients in a blender, or whisk in a bowl.

SERVING SUGGESTION

Serve with a scoop of chocolate or vanilla soy ice cream in addition to the Peanut Butter Cinnamon Topping, and garnish with toasted shredded coconut and chocolate chips.

Quickie Banana Almond Sundae

2 SUNDAES

2 big scoops vanilla soy ice cream

1 banana, sliced

2 Tbsp almond butter

2 or more dried sweet cherries

....

In each of two dishes, portion out a big scoop of vanilla soy ice cream, then sliced banana, and almond butter. Top each with a dried cherry—a natural replacement for those artificially colored, sugary maraschino cherries.

Martha's Glazed Nuts

2 CUPS

It's OK to share this with your friends!

2 cups walnut or pecan halves

2 Tbsp nondairy margarine

¼ cup maple syrup

2 Tbsp molasses sugar (see page 28) or brown sugar

¼ tsp sea salt

....

Put nuts in a heated skillet and stir until they are toasted and lightly browned. Add margarine and toss nuts to coat and brown a little more. Stir in maple syrup, sugar, and salt. Reduce flame and stir until nuts are coated and liquid is gone. Let cool. They are best eaten within three weeks, but they probably won't last three days.

SERVING SUGGESTION

These nuts make a simple but unforgettable gift, packed in a decorative container or jar.

Chocolate French Silk Lingerie Pie

This dessert has a very high "Ooh la la" factor. It's quite rich, so reserve it for special occasions only!

Chocolate Cookie Pie Crust

- 1 stick ($\frac{1}{2}$ cup) nondairy margarine
- $\frac{3}{4}$ cup sugar
- 1 tsp vanilla extract
- $1\frac{1}{4}$ cups unbleached pastry flour
- $\frac{1}{4}$ cup unsweetened cocoa powder
- $\frac{1}{8}$ tsp baking soda
- $\frac{1}{8}$ tsp sea salt
- $\frac{1}{2}$ cup semisweet chocolate or chocolate chips, cut into $\frac{1}{8}$-inch bits

....

Preheat oven to 350°F. Leave the margarine at room temperature until slightly softened. Place the margarine, sugar, and vanilla in a mixing bowl, and cream together until smooth. Mix in flour, cocoa powder, baking soda, and salt. Stir in chocolate bits. Gather the dough into a ball. On a lightly floured surface, roll out the dough into a 10-inch round, $\frac{1}{4}$ inch thick. Place dough in a 9-inch pie tin, and bake for 12–15 minutes. Let cool before adding filling.

Silk Lingerie Pie Filling

- 1 stick ($\frac{1}{2}$ cup) nondairy margarine
- $\frac{3}{4}$ cup sugar
- 2 tsp vanilla extract

1½ squares unsweetened chocolate

¾ cup soy milk

½ cup canned coconut milk

1 Tbsp agar flakes

· ·

Leave the margarine at room temperature until slightly softened. Place the margarine, sugar, and vanilla in a mixing
bowl and cream together until smooth.

Melt the chocolate in a saucepan over low heat or in a
double boiler. Remove from heat.

In a saucepan, combine soy milk, coconut milk, and
agar flakes. Bring mixture to a boil, lower heat, and simmer
2 minutes, stirring as it thickens. Pour into the bowl with
the margarine-sugar mixture, add the melted chocolate, and
beat until well mixed. Pour into cooled Chocolate Cookie
Pie Crust. Let pie sit until it comes to room temperature.
Chill in refrigerator for at least an hour.

SERVING SUGGESTION

*Top each slice of pie with Vanilla Crème (page 301) and
chocolate chips.*

Sam's Vegan Cheesecake

9-INCH CHEESECAKE

In honor of the publisher of Shambhala Publications, Sam Bercholtz (a.k.a. The Man).

SERVING SUGGESTION

Top with fresh seasonal berries or Martha's Glazed Nuts (page 282). Place a mint leaf on the corner of a slice for a simple, pretty garnish.

Crust

- 2 cups granola (your favorite)
- 4 Tbsp nondairy margarine
- 2 Tbsp sugar

Filling

- 1 cup (8 oz) soy sour cream (Tofutti brand)
- 16 oz soy cream cheese (Tofutti brand)
- 1 cup sugar
- 2 Tbsp unbleached flour
- 1 Tbsp lemon juice
- 1 tsp vanilla extract
- 1 tsp sea salt

Preheat oven to 325°F. Grind granola in a blender to the consistency of coarse flour. Melt margarine in a small pot. Mix granola and sugar in a bowl, and stir in melted margarine. Press crust mixture into a 9-inch spring-form pan or deep dish pie tin.

Blend filling ingredients in blender and pour into crust. Bake for 20–25 minutes until just golden brown.

Lulu's Lemon Cake

8 x 8–INCH CAKE

Here in Southern California we have a lot of lemon trees, and in the Palm Springs area everyone has at least one in their yard. There are so many lemons in the winter that most just get composted. We've taken to freezing the juice for later use. Let them eat lemon cake—year round!

1 cup unbleached or whole wheat pastry flour

1½ tsp baking powder

½ cup nondairy margarine

1 cup maple syrup

grated rind of 1 lemon

1 Egg Substitute

Egg Substitute

2 Tbsp vital gluten flour (see page 22)

½ tsp baking powder

2 Tbsp water

Glaze

¼ cup maple syrup

juice of 1 lemon

. . . .

Preheat oven to 350°F. Oil and flour an 8 x 8–inch square baking pan.

Mix 1 cup flour with baking powder in mixing bowl. Melt margarine in a small saucepan. Remove from heat, and stir in 1 cup maple syrup and lemon rind.

To make the Egg Substitute, mix together the vital gluten flour, baking powder, and water. (Don't let it sit too long before you use it.) Whisk the Egg Substitute into the maple syrup mixture. Fold liquid mixture into flour mixture.

Pour into prepared baking pan, and bake for 25–30 minutes.

While cake is baking, combine ¼ cup maple syrup with the juice from the lemon. After removing cake from oven and while it is still warm, prick top of cake with fork, then pour the maple–lemon juice mixture over it. Let cake cool in pan before serving.

Pineapple Upside Down Cake

9- OR 10-INCH ROUND
CAKE

VARIATION

*Use grilled fresh pineapple
slices instead of canned slices.
Lightly brush with sunflower
or safflower oil before grilling
on outdoor grill.*

¼ cup nondairy margarine

½ cup brown sugar (such as Sucanat brand granulated
cane juice, Rapadura organic sugar, or molasses
sugar)

1 lb 10 oz can sliced pineapple

10–12 dried sweet cherries

14–16 pecan halves

1½ cup unbleached flour

2½ tsp baking powder

¼ tsp sea salt

⅓ cup sunflower or safflower oil

1 cup sugar

6 oz firm silken tofu (aseptic package)

½ cup pineapple or orange juice

1 tsp vanilla extract

½ tsp lemon extract

Preheat oven to 350°F.

Mash sugar with margarine (using a fork or your fingers)
on bottom of 9- or 10-inch round pan. Arrange pineapple
slices in bottom of pan, and place a cherry in the center of
each pineapple slice. Place pecan halves around spaces between pineapple slices.

In a mixing bowl, combine flour, baking powder, and sea salt. Purée the rest of the ingredients in a blender. Mix liquid into dry ingredients, and spoon batter evenly over pineapple slices.

Bake for 35–40 minutes. Let cool on rack, then invert onto a platter so that cake is upside down. Serve with Sweet Ginger Cream (page 303) and sweet dreams. . . .

Chocolate Mint Holiday Balls

2 DOZEN

½ cup nondairy margarine

¼ cup sugar

½ tsp vanilla extract

1½ tsp peppermint extract

1¼ cups unbleached flour

½ tsp baking soda

⅓ cup chocolate chips

1 Egg Substitute

Egg Substitute

2 Tbsp vital gluten flour (see page 22)

½ tsp baking powder

2 Tbsp water

Preheat oven to 350°F. Beat softened margarine and sugar until well blended.

Make the Egg Substitute by mixing together the vital gluten flour, baking powder, and water. Beat the Egg Substitute into the margarine-sugar mixture, and add the vanilla and peppermint extracts.

Combine flour and baking soda in a separate bowl, and then add gradually to margarine-sugar mixture, mixing thoroughly. Add chocolate chips.

Measure approximately 2 teaspoons of dough, roll it into a ball, and place it on cookie sheet. Continue with rest of dough, placing balls 2 inches apart. Bake until golden brown, about 10 minutes.

Chocolate Cherry Cookies

3 DOZEN

2 cups unbleached or whole wheat pastry flour

2 tsp baking soda

1 tsp sea salt

1½ cups sugar

½ cup maple syrup

½ cup nondairy margarine or vegetable shortening

½ cup sunflower oil

½ cup canned coconut milk or soy milk

2 tsp vanilla extract

¾ cup pecan or walnut pieces

¾ cup chocolate chips

½ cup dried sweet cherries (chopped if large)

....

Preheat oven to 300°F. Combine flour, baking soda, and sea salt in a mixing bowl. In a separate bowl, cream sugar, maple syrup, margarine, oil, coconut milk and vanilla. Gradually mix in dry ingredients. Stir in pecans, chocolate chips, and dried cherries. Drop in spoonfuls on cookie sheet and bake for 20 minutes.

VARIATION

Omit chocolate chips and cherries, and substitute ¾ cup chopped dates and 2 teaspoons ground cardamom.

Jungle Boogie Bars

16–20 BARS

These bars have been making customers boogie for a few years now. Bake some of these and boogie on down down with your baby.

2 cups unbleached flour

1 cup rolled oats

1 Tbsp baking powder

½ tsp sea salt

1 cup sliced almonds

½ cup shredded coconut

½ cup chocolate chips

2 cups maple syrup

6 oz firm silken tofu (aseptic package)

1 ripe banana

½ cup saffower or sunflower oil

½ cup vegetable shortening

1 Tbsp vanilla

Preheat oven to 375°F. Mix flour, oats, baking powder, salt, almonds, coconut, and chocolate chips together in a large bowl. Purée maple syrup, tofu, banana, oil, shortening, and vanilla in a blender. Combine liquid ingredients with dry mixture. Pour into an oiled 13 x 9–inch baking pan, and bake 35–40 minutes. Let cool before cutting into bars.

Gertrude's Ya-Ya Apple Strudel

2 STRUDELS, 6–8 SERVINGS

A quick, simple preparation. This strudel is more like a Neapolitan style than a traditional rolled strudel made with a butter dough, which adds a nice flair for presentation while still remaining easy to make. If it doesn't make you "ya-ya," it will certainly make you yodel for more.

⅔ cup sugar

1 tsp cinnamon

4 medium apples

1 Tbsp lemon juice

2 tsp lemon zest (see page 48)

1 cup ground toasted hazelnuts

¾ cup dried cranberries

1 lb filo dough

¼ cup sunflower or safflower oil

1½ cups Vanilla Crème (page 301)

· ·

Preheat oven to 375°F. Mix sugar and cinnamon together, and set aside.

Peel and core apples, and cut into ⅛-inch slices. If the peel is soft, you can leave it on if you like. Toss apples with lemon juice and zest.

Unwrap filo and remove about 12 sheets. Put the rest back in the plastic bag and seal. Cut filo in half lengthwise. On a lightly oiled cookie sheet, place 4 half sheets of filo and brush with oil. Sprinkle ground hazelnuts on filo, leaving a 1-inch margin all around. Arrange sliced apples on top of nuts, and sprinkle with cinnamon sugar and dried cranberries.

Repeat layering of 4 sheets of filo and apples. End with 4 sheets of filo on top, and brush with oil. Sprinkle top with a little cinnamon/sugar mixture.

Repeat with rest of ingredients to make the second strudel. Bake for 25 minutes or until golden brown. Let cool slightly before serving. Top each serving with a spoonful of Vanilla Crème.

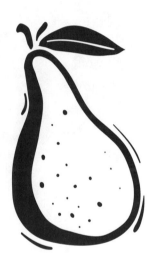

Eleni's California Baklava

We like all kinds of nuts in
California, as I'm sure you've
heard.

1½ cups finely chopped raw almonds

1½ cups finely chopped raw cashews

1½ cups finely chopped walnuts

1½ tsp cinnamon

¼ cup nondairy margarine

¼ cup sunflower or safflower oil

1 lb box filo dough

1 cup maple syrup

¼ cup orange juice

1 Tbsp lemon juice

2 tsp lemon zest (see page 48)

2 tsp orange zest (see page 48)

....

Preheat oven to 350°F. Mix chopped almonds, cashews, and
walnuts with cinnamon. In a separate bowl, melt margarine
and combine with oil.

Remove filo dough sheets and unroll, dividing into three
stacks. Dip a pastry brush into the margarine-oil mixture
and lightly brush it onto a 13 x 9 x 2–inch baking dish.

Place the first stack in the baking dish, and lift the
sheets to brush with the margarine-oil mixture on every second sheet. Sprinkle with a third of the nut mixture. Take
half of the second stack of filo, and repeat the procedure
until you end up with the last stack of filo. Brush remaining
margarine-oil mixture over top.

Bake for 30 minutes, then reduce oven temperature to 300°F and bake for another 30 minutes.

Meanwhile, in a saucepan, heat maple syrup, orange juice, lemon juice, and lemon and orange zest, and simmer for 15 minutes.

Let baklava cool just enough to cut into 24 pieces. Pour the warm maple mixture over the sliced baklava while still warm. You may serve it slightly warm or at room temperature. Don't cover it tightly with plastic wrap or put it in a sealed container, as that will make the filo soft and not crispy; but you can always slightly rewarm it in a conventional oven to revive the texture.

SERVING SUGGESTION

Serve with 1½ Sambuca Crème (page 302)

Juan's Flan

6 SERVINGS

⅔ cup maple syrup

2 tsp orange zest

1 quart soy milk

¼ cup agar flakes

3 Tbsp kuzu or arrowroot, dissolved in ½ cup cold water

1 Tbsp vanilla extract

cinnamon for garnish

···

In a saucepan, heat ⅓ cup maple syrup and simmer until reduced to about ¼ cup. Add orange zest, remove from heat, and set aside.

Combine soy milk and agar flakes in a saucepan, and simmer until agar is dissolved. Add kuzu dissolved in water, ⅓ cup maple syrup, and vanilla. Stir over high heat until mixture thickens and then comes to a boil. Remove from heat.

In individual 1-cup soufflé dishes, portion the reduced maple syrup–orange zest mixture. Fill dishes slowly with thickened soy milk mixture. Let set, then refrigerate 2 hours.

Invert each flan dish onto a small serving plate. Sprinkle with cinnamon to garnish.

Apple Pudding

2 SERVINGS

This is a simple, great dessert if you are trying to get the sugar cravings out of your diet—and it's good for babies and young children too.

1 large Granny Smith apple

1½ cups water

1 tsp kuzu, dissolved in ¼ cup water

Chop apple into 1-inch cubes. Bring water to a boil in a saucepan and add apple. Turn heat to medium-low and simmer, uncovered, 5–7 minutes. Stir in kuzu dissolved in ¼ cup water. Stir until thickened, about 2–3 minutes. Let cool slightly, then purée in blender.

VARIATIONS

- *Add ¼ teaspoon cinnamon when simmering apple.*
- *Add ½ teaspoon lemon zest along with the kuzu.*
- *Substitute pear for apple.*

Japanese Jiggy Jell

4–6 SERVINGS

This dessert is made from agar, a clear, clean sea vegetable that gels when cooked, like commercial Jell-O. Jell-O and similar products contain gelatin, which is made from meat-industry by-products (hooves, bones, and skin). I learned this when I was little, and it stopped me cold from ever eating another Jell-O cube. Give kids the choice, they'll opt for this version anytime!

1 quart apple juice

⅓ cup agar flakes

1 Tbsp kuzu, dissolved in ¼ cup water

½ tsp almond extract

pinch sea salt

2 cups fresh fruit, such as berries or chopped peaches or pears, for garnish

....

Combine apple juice and agar flakes in a saucepan. Place on the stove over medium heat and stir until mixture boils and agar is dissolved. Add kuzu dissolved in ¼ cup water and continue stirring. Lower flame and simmer while stirring for about 10 minutes, until liquid is clear. Stir in almond extract. Remove from heat.

Pour into a heatproof bowl or individual serving dishes. Let sit until firm, and chill in refrigerator at least 2 hours before serving. Garnish with fresh fruit.

VARIATIONS

• *Add different extracts (such as coconut, lemon, or cherry) or fresh lemon or orange zest.*
• *Add berries directly to mixture after removing from heat, then pour into serving dishes.*

Chestnut Yam Pudding Cream

4 SERVINGS

Another great dessert for sweet cravings without the intense sugar.

2 medium yams, chopped in 1-inch cubes

2 cups cooked peeled chestnuts

   pinch sea salt

2 Tbsp barley malt or maple syrup (optional)

1 tsp vanilla extract

½ tsp cinnamon

½ cup chopped roasted almonds or pecans

....

Place chopped yams, chestnuts, and sea salt in a saucepan, and fill with water to cover by 2 inches. Bring to boil, then turn to medium-low heat and let simmer 20–25 minutes, until soft. Stir in rest of ingredients. Remove from heat and let cool. Purée in blender and serve in bowls, topped with the chopped roasted nuts.

Vanilla Crème

1 ½ CUPS

1 box firm silken tofu (aseptic package)

¾ cup soy milk

⅓ cup sugar or maple syrup

1 Tbsp vanilla extract

....

Purée all ingredients in blender until smooth and creamy.
Serve as a topping for desserts such as ice cream, fresh
fruit, and pastry.

Sambuca Crème

1 ½ CUPS

Sambuca is a liqueur pro-
duced in Italy, similar to the
Greek ouzo, that licorice-like
drink you may have tried at
Greek restaurants. It is usually after drinking ouzo that
the restaurant patrons start
yelling *"Oopa!"* and begin to
break plates.

Follow recipe for Vanilla Crème (page 301), and add 2–3
tablespoons Sambuca.

VARIATION

Add ¼ teaspoon anise seed extract instead of Sambuca.

Sweet Ginger Cream

1 ½ CUPS

1 box silken firm tofu (aseptic package)

¾ cup soy milk

⅓ cup sugar or maple syrup

1 tsp vanilla extract

1 tsp grated fresh ginger

Purée all ingredients in a blender. Slather on anything sweet for anyone who loves ginger.

specialty drinks

*H*ere are some favorite drinks we now serve at our restaurants or have served throughout the years.

Native Iced Tea

APPROX. I QUART

1 quart water

6 bags hibiscus tea, or herbal tea blend with hibiscus

1–2 cups apple juice

fresh orange slices

fresh mint sprigs

···

Put water in a pitcher and add tea bags. Let steep in refrigerator for at least 1 hour (longer is OK). Remove tea bags. Add apple juice, and serve in glasses with a fresh orange slice and mint sprig in each.

VARIATION

Use any kind of fruity herbal tea with natural flavors. Stay away from those strong, overpowering, artificially sweetened herbal teas.

Mexican Hot Chocolate

2 CUPS

2 Tbsp cocoa powder

1 Tbsp sugar or maple syrup

1 tsp vanilla extract

¼ tsp cinnamon

2 pinches sea salt

2 cups soy milk

· ·

In a small saucepan, mix together cocoa powder, sugar, vanilla, cinnamon, and sea salt. Slowly whisk in soy milk. Heat over medium heat until almost boiling. Pour in cups and serve.

CHOCOLATE

Chocolate in its origins in South America was always used in savory (not sweet) dishes (see Seitan Olé Molé, page 221). The Mayans and Aztecs of Mexico believed that the God of Agriculture provided the cacao seed from Paradise. As a beverage, chocolate was created when Cortés brought cacao beans to Spain in the 1500s. The Spaniards added sugar and cinnamon and heated the brew to improve the taste of the otherwise bitter drink. And when the Dutch got hold of it, they added milk.

Guru Chai

6–8 SERVINGS

Chai is the word for "tea" in many eastern European and Asian countries. This recipe is based on a version commonly prepared in India.

3-inch piece fresh ginger, peeled and cut into ¼-inch slices

10 cups water

three 3-inch cinnamon sticks

½ tsp black peppercorns

6 cloves

10 cardamom pods

4 bags Earl Grey tea

4 bags Darjeeling or other black tea

1 cup sugar

3 cups soy milk

• •

In a large soup pot, bring water with ginger and spices to a boil, and let simmer 20 minutes. Remove pot from heat and add tea bags. Let steep 30 minutes. Strain out spices and tea bags by pouring through strainer. Add sugar and stir to dissolve; then add soy milk. Serve hot.

VARIATIONS

• *Add the sugar but not the soy milk, and store in containers in the refrigerator. Heat portions as needed, and add soy milk as desired when heating.*
• *In summer, serve chilled over ice, and float ¼ cup of soy milk on top of each serving.*

Palm Desert Date Shake

1 SERVING

Dates are significant to two of our restaurant locales. Palm Desert, California, was named after the groves of date palms that used to encompass the city. Although most of the groves have succumbed to walled condominium and housing developments, Palm Desert recently established a date grove as part of its city park in order to preserve its namesake. Palm Springs is Palm Desert's sister city to the west. It was named after the Washingtonia species of palms, which line the spring- and waterfall-rich canyons that surround the city.

8 dates, pitted
1 cup soy milk
1 Tbsp raw almonds
¼ cup orange juice
½ tsp vanilla extract
1 cup ice

Purée all ingredients in a blender.

VARIATIONS

- *Add ½ medium banana.*
- *Substitute 1 scoop vanilla soy ice cream for ice.*

El Choco-Banana

I got the idea for this recipe
while on my first surfing trip,
near Puerta Vallarta, Mexico.
It tastes great after lots of
sun and salt water.

1 banana
1 scoop chocolate soy ice cream
1 Tbsp ground almonds
1¼ cups soy milk
½ tsp vanilla extract
⅛ tsp cinnamon
cocoa powder for garnish

Purée all ingredients in a blender. Pour into glass and garnish
top of drink with cocoa powder.

Crystal Blue Persuasion

There is something kind of nice and surreal about the way you taste the lavender in this drink. It's as if it's not from your tastebuds—it's almost from your forehead. Try it!

1 banana

1 cup ice

2 Tbsp blueberries

2 small pieces crystallized ginger

¼ tsp lavender flowers

¾ cup soymilk

blueberries for garnish

Purée all ingredients (except garnish) in a blender. Garnish with 2–3 fresh blueberries.

LAVENDER IS FOR LOVERS

Lavender seems to have originated in Greece, and upon arrival in France it apparently turned the French into a nation of lovers, as the aroma does seem to have amorous effects! The cuisine of Provence in southern France is especially noted for its use of lavender.

For centuries the oil has been extracted from the gorgeous purple flowers and used as an antiseptic for minor scrapes, cuts, and burns. The aroma aids in soothing and calming the emotions, thereby helping to relieve anxiety and insomnia.

The dried flowers are used in cooking. It is important to use very little, as a bitter taste can be imparted when too much is used. It is often steeped or added in small amounts as part of a liquid ingredient when added to recipes. It really "perfumes" rather than "flavors" a dish or drink.

Lavender Lemonade

1 QUART

4 lemons (rind and juice)

1 cup sugar

1 quart water

1 tsp lavender flowers

Peel rind from lemons with a sharp paring knife, trying not to get include too much of the white pith, and cut into ¼-inch strips. Place rind strips in a bowl, cover them with sugar, and let sit for 1 hour, as this releases the oils from the rind.

Boil water and pour over lemon rind and sugar. Add lavender flowers and let steep 20 minutes.

Juice the lemons. Strain the rinds and lavender flours from the mixture, and add the lemon juice.

Refrigerate and let chill well. Serve over ice.

Mocha Frappé

2 SERVINGS

1½ cups coffee, chilled or at room temperature

½ cup soy milk

2 Tbsp cocoa powder

1 Tbsp sugar or maple syrup

1 cup ice

cocoa powder for garnish

....

Blend all ingredients in a blender. Garnish with cocoa powder.

Cranberry Shrub

8 SERVINGS

This recipe is based on an old colonial drink, which would have been spiked with rum or brandy. Do what you want! Here is the basic recipe.

1 quart cranberry juice, fruit-juice–sweetened

½ cup lemon juice

2 tsp lime zest

1 pint lime or raspberry sorbet

2 cups sparkling water or club soda

....

In a mixing bowl or large pitcher, mix together cranberry juice, lemon juice, and lime zest. Fill eight glasses halfway. Add a small scoop of sorbet to each serving; then top off with ¼ cup of soda water.

Roasted Barley Tea

2 SERVINGS

This is the ultimate everyday tea. It has a roasty flavor and a nice vitamin and mineral content, which include B vitamins and vitamin E. It's caffeine- and calorie-free and contains secret properties that we've sworn not to reveal! It's great hot—and in the summer you'll crave it chilled. Find barley tea in Asian markets or in health food stores. Check our web site for more references.

2 tsp loose roasted barley tea

3 cups boiling water

....

Bring water to boil in a saucepan, add tea, and let simmer 5 minutes. Alternatively, you can brew it in a press pot. Strain through a fine sieve and serve.

in closing

Compassion for all beings (*daya*) is necessary for divine realization, for God Himself is overflowing with this quality. Those with a tender heart can put themselves in the place of others, feel their suffering, and try to alleviate it.

—Paramahansa Yogananda

index

adzuki (azuki) beans, 17, 52
agar, 17
almonds
    bars, with coconut, 292
    and currant chutney, toasted, 88
amaranth, 18, 57–58
Anaheim chilies, 19
appetizers, snacks
    cauliflower crudité with sesame curry dip, 146
    cucumber bites, 143
    edamame, 135
    eggplant and roasted pepper purée, 144
    guacamole, 147
    hummus, 136
    kim chee (pickled cabbage), 148
    mushrooms, stuffed, 145
    nachos, 149
    salsa, roasted garlic and hummus, 137
    spanakopita, 141–42
    tapenade, 140
    tempeh pâté, 138–39
    tempeh with peanut sauce, 150
apple cider vinegar, 18
apples
    Apple Pudding, 298
    apple-almond gelatin, 299
    date-wrapped "caramel," 278
    strudel, 293–94
appliances, recommended, 35–36
arame, 18, 267
arrowroot, 18
artichokes, 251–52
asparagus soup, 162

Atomic Split Pea soup, 156
avocado, 18, 147

Bagel E, 210
Bagel No Lox, 209
Baja Enchilada sauce, 119
baking pans, bake wear, 33, 49
baklava, 295–96
Bali Surf Burger, 198
balsamic vinaigrette, 104
balsamic vinegar, 18
Banana Coconut Chutney, 226
bananas
    banana chutney, 226
    banana salsa, 131
    shake, with chocolate, 309
    shake, with lavender, 310
bancha tea, 18
barbecue sauce, 128
barley, 58
    malt syrup, 18
    roasted, tea using, 19, 314
Basic Balsamic Vinaigrette, 104
Basic Tofu Marinade, 80
basil chiffonade, 45
basmati rice, 59
BBQ Love Burger, 204
beans and peas, overview, 52–56. *See also specific beans*
Béchamel sauce, 218
beet and potato salad, 177
Bessie's (Thank-You) BBQ Sauce, 128
beverages
    chai, 307

beverages (*continued*)
    frappé, mocha, 312
    hot chocolate, Mexican-style, 306
    lemonade, with lavender, 311
    shake, banana with lavender, 310
    shake, chocolate-banana, 309
    shake, date, 308
    shrub, cranberry, 313
    tea, iced, 305
    tea, roasted barley, 19, 314
black beans
    Black Bean Soup with Masa Balls, 159–60
    how to cook, 52
    salads, 176
Black Creek Ranch Dressing, 113
blackening spice, 101
blackening technique, 44
black-eyed peas, 52
blanching technique, 44
bowls, recommended, 33
breads
    corn bread, 265
    lavosh, 24
    naan, 266
brests. *See* soy brests
broths, stocks, 65, 70
brown rice, sweet, 59
brunch dishes. *See* side dishes
Brunoise technique, 45
buckwheat
    general information, 58
    groats (kasha), 23
    soba noodles, 27
burgers. *See* sandwiches, wraps
burritos
    breakfast, brunch, 202
    seitan and black bean, 201
Butternut Squash and Lemon Grass Bisque, 163
Bye Bye Barnum Black Bean Salad, 176

cabbage
    pickled (kim chee), 148
    rolls, 234–35
Caesar salad, 169

Caesar's Vegan salad dressing, 112
cakes and cookies. *See* desserts, sweets
Caldo Verde (Portuguese Greens Soup), 157
California Caesar salad, 169
California Caesar Wrap with Tempeh, 197
capers, 19
Caramelized Onions, 102
cardamom, 19
carnivore, defined, 11
Carrot Cake with Dream Cheese Frosting, 272–73
carrot tops, miso-lemon flavored, 96
cashew nuts
    curried crunch, 91
    nondairy cheese from, 97
Cauliflower Crudité with Sesame Curry Dip, 146
cereals. *See* grains
chai
    Chai Pumpkin Pie, 275
    recipe, 307
chard, sautéed with onions, 249
cheese, nondairy
    cashew- and tahini-based, 97
    in cheesecake, 285
    cream cheese, soy, 27–28
    feta, tofu-based, 99
    in nachos, 149
    ricotta, tofu-based, 98
cheesecloth, 36
chestnuts, 19
    Chestnut Yam Pudding Cream, 300
    stuffing, with cranberries, 247
"chicken" brests. *See* soy brests
Chicken Fried Steak, 230
chickpeas. *See* garbanzo beans
chiffonade technique, 45
chili peppers, 19
chili powder, 20
Chinese "Save the Chicken" Salad, 179
Chinese-style tofu, 79
chipotle, 19, 100
chocolate
    cake with peanut butter cinnamon topping, 279
    Chocolate Cherry Cookies, 291
    Chocolate Cookie Pie Crust, 283

Chocolate French Silk Lingerie Pie, 283–84
Chocolate Mint Holiday Balls, 290
cocoa, Free Trade, 222
El Choco-Banana shake, 309
history, 306
hot, Mexican-style, 306
mocha frappé, 312
seitan with molé sauce, 221–22
chopping, 45–46
chowder, corn, 158
Ciao Bella Burger, 199
cilantro, 20
citrus. See fruits
cocoa, Free Trade, 222
coconut
almond coconut oat bats, 292
Coconut Groove Rice, 253
coconut milk, 20
dried, 20
cole slaw, Thai-style, 188
condiments, accompaniments
blackening spice, 101
capers, 19
carrot tops, miso-lemon flavored, 96
cashews, curried, 91
chutney, almond and currant, 88
chutney, banana coconut, 226
croutons, garlic-flavored, 92
garlic cloves, roasted, 86
gomasio (sesame salt), 95
onions, caramelized, 102
pickles, cucumber, 89
relish, cranberry orange, 93
salsa, tomatillo-chili, 100
sesame seeds, toasted, 94
Tofu Ricotta, 98
converted rice, 59
cookies. See cakes and cookies
cooking methods and times
beans, 52–56
glossary of techniques, 44–46
glossary of terms, 37–43
grains, 62
coriander, 20

corn
chowder, 158
corn bread, 265
corn flour, cornmeal, 20
general information, 58
Masa Balls, 160
cornstarch, 20
Country Croutons, 92
couscous, 20–21
cranberries
Cranberry Chestnut Stuffing, 247
Cranberry Orange Relish, 93
Cranberry Shrub, 313
Cravin' Corn Chowder, 158
cream cheese, soy. See cheese, nondairy
Creamy Wild Mushroom sauce, 124
croutons, garlic-flavored, 92
crusts, pie
for cheesecake, 285
chocolate cookie, 283
flaky, 277
Crystal Blue Persuasion, 310
cucumbers
cucumber bites, 143
Cucumber Quick Pickles, 89
general information, 21
cumin, 21
currant chutney, 88
curry
Curried Cashew Crunch, 91
curry, mung bean, 225–26
Curry Lime Vinaigrette, 114
curry powder, 21
curry sauce, 117
cutting boards, 46

daikon
general information, 21
pickles from, 90
date shake, 308
desserts, sweets
almond coconut oat bars, 292
apple pudding, 298
apple strudel, 293–94

desserts, sweets (*continued*)
   apple-almond gelatin, 299
   apples, date-wrapped "caramel," 278
   baklava, 295–96
   banana cream pie, 276
   banana-almond sundae, 281
   carrot cake, 272–73
   cheesecake, 285
   chestnut-yam pudding, 300
   chocolate cake with peanut butter cinnamon
      topping, 279–80
   chocolate cherry cookies, 291
   chocolate-mint cookies, 290
   chocolate silk pie, 283–84
   flaky pie crust, 277
   flan, 297
   key lime parfait, 274
   lemon cake, 286–87
   nuts, glazed, 282
   pineapple upside down cake, 288–89
   pumpkin pie, chai-flavored, 275
   vanilla topping, 301
diagonal slices, 47
dicing, 46
Dream Cheese Frosting, 273
dry ingredients, measuring, 49

East Indian Onion Bread (Naan), 266
edamame (green soybeans)
   general information, 21, 54
   in Japanese-style fried rice, 254
   preparing, 135
eggplant
   Eggplant Rollatini, 229
   moussaka, 218–19
   and roasted pepper purée (ivar), 144
"egg" salad, tofu, 178
Egg Substitute recipe, 22, 286
El Bruncho burrito, 202
Eleni's California Baklava, 295–96
Elephant Chocolate Cake, 279
enchilada sauce, 119
entrées
   baked tofu with quinoa and yams, 223

cabbage rolls, 234–35
chicken fried steak, 230
eggplant rolls, 229
enchilada stacks, 212–13
fajitas, 231
Hungarian Goulash, 217
Italian Ground Around, 75
Jamaican-style pasta primavera, 241
Jamaican-style roasted soy brests, 242
Moroccan-style seitan, 232
moussaka, 218–19
mung bean curry, 225–26
rice and mixed vegetables, 214
seitan Stroganoff, 220
seitan with molé sauce, 221–22
soy brest barbecue, 227–28
soy brest grill, 77
steamed tofu with peanut sauce, 236
sweet and sour soy nuggets, 237
Taco Meat, 75
Tempeh Provençale, 216
tempeh scaloppine with shallot mushroom
   gravy, 215
Thai-style stir-fry, 233
tofu with spinach and Hollandaise sauce, 224
vegetable pot pies, 238
equipment overview, 33–36

Farrah's Fattoush, 182
fats, oils, overview, 25–29
Fellini's Dream salad, 180
feta, tofu, 99
filo, 22
fish. *See* Tuno (tuna alternative)
Flaky Pie Crust, 277
Flamed Banana Salsa, 131
Flaming Fajitas, 231
flan, 297
Fleetwood Macaroni Salad, 183
flours
   corn flour, 20
   gluten flour, 22–23
   measuring, 49
   rice flour, 26

Fred's Corn Bread, 265
French Love Bites, 139
Fresh Asparagus Soup, 162
fried rice, 254, 255
frostings, toppings
    "dream" cheese, 273
    ginger cream, 303
    Sambuca cream, 302
    vanilla cream, 301
fruits
    citrus zest, 31
    coconut, 20
    curry lime vinaigrette, 114
    key lime parfait, 274
    lemonade, with lavender, 311
    mango lime vinaigrette, 107
    ponzu, 109
    sesame orange vinaigrette, 110
    Watermelon Chill salad, 186
Fun Mung Curry, 225–26

Gandhi Bowl, 214
Gandhi's Curry Sauce, 117
garbanzo beans (chickpeas), 22
    cooking times and methods, 52
    hummus recipe, 136
garlic
    croutons, garlic-flavored, 92
    garlic-lemon salad dressing, 106
    Garlic Toast, 87
    roasted, 86
    slicing, 47
garnishes, 39–40
gazpacho, 154
gelatin, cruelty-free, 17–18
Gertrude's Ya-Ya Apple Strudel, 293–94
Get Yo' Greens, 259
ginger, 22
ginger cream topping, 303
glaze, for lemon cake, 286
gluten flour, 22
Gomasio (sesame salt), 95
Good Karma Sarma: Cabbage Rolls, 234–35
Gorgeous Greek Salad, 181

grains, 18–20, 57–62. See also specific grains
    how to cook, 61–62
grating, 46
Greek Lemon Garlic Dressing, 106
Greek salad, 181
green beans with Portobello mushrooms, 257
Green Goddess salad dressing, 105
green onions, 23
green pea soup, 161
greens
    basic recipe, 259
    in Portuguese soup, 157
Green Tea Sesame Sauce, 127
groats, 58
Guacamole, 147
Guru Chai, 307

half-moon slices, 47
Harry's Hummus, 136
"heaping" spoonfuls, 49
Hearty Broth, 194
hemp seeds, 23
herbs de Provence, 23
hijiki, 23, 268
Hollandaise Sauce, 133
Hollywood Bowl, The, 236
Hot Italian sandwich, 193
hummus, 136
Hungarian Goulash, 217

ingredients, basic, glossary of, 17–31
In Thyme for Breakfast Potatoes, 246
Iron Yam salad, 174
isoflavones, 54
Italian Ground Around (soy protein), 75
Italian Salsa, 120
Italian sandwich, hot, 193
ivar (eggplant and roasted pepper purée), 144

jalapeño (pepper), 19
Jamaican Jerk Marinade, 130
Japanese Fried Rice, 255
Japanese Jiggy Jell, 299
Japanese Soy Citrus Dressing (Ponzu), 109

jasmine rice, 59
Jerked "Save the Chicken," 242
jerk marinade, 130
José y Jesus' Jicama Salad, 173
Juan's Flan, 297
julienne slices, 47
Jungle Boogie Bars, 292

kasha. *See* buckwheat
Kasha Varnishkas, 264
Key Lime Parfait, 274
kidney beans, 52
kim chee (pickled cabbage), 148
Kissed French Toast, 244
knives, recommended, 33, 36
koji, 25
kombu, 23, 56, 61
Korean Tacos, 206
kuzu, 23–24

lavender
    Lavender Lemonade, 311
    uses for, 310
lavosh, 24
leavening agents, 24
Le Benedict Florentine, 224
lecithin, 54
Leek 'n' Lemon side dish, 263
lemon-garlic salad dressing, 106
lemon grass, 24
Lemon Potato Salad, 184
lentils
    how to cook, 52–53
    soups using, 153, 154
lima beans, 53
lotus root, 24
Love Portion Green Beans, 257
Loving Lentil soup, 154
Lulu's Lemon Cake, 286–87

macaroni salad, 183
Mad Cowboy barbecue, 227–28
Madison's Garden Dressing, 115

Mama's Mexican Rice, 256
Mango Lime Vinaigrette, 107
Manilow's Minestrone, 164–65
maple syrup, 24–25
margarine, vegan, 25
marinades
    jerk marinade, 130
    Moroccan, 132
    for soy chunks, brests, 76
    for tofu, 80–81
marinara sauce, 118
Martha's Glazed Nuts, 282
Masa Balls, 160
mayonnaise, vegan
    sources, 25
    in tartar sauce, 129
    in Thousand Island dressing, 111
measurements, equivalents for, 50
measurement utensils, 33, 49
meat alternatives. *See* seitan; soy protein
    textures; tempeh
Mecca Azteca Salad, 167
Mexican Hot Chocolate, 306
milk
    coconut, 20
    soy, 28
millet, 25, 58
mincing technique, 46
minestrone, 164–65
miso, 25–26
    Miso Lemon Carrot tops, 96
    miso soup, 151
Mocha Frappé, 312
Moroccan marinade, 132
moussaka, 218–19
Mr. Weld's Banana Cream Pie, 276
mung beans, 26
    in curry, 225–26
    how to use, 53
mushrooms
    with green beans, 257
    shallot mushroom gravy, 125
    stuffed, 145

wild mushroom salad, 168
wild mushroom sauce, 124

Naan (East Indian Onion Bread), 266
Nacho Gazpacho, 155
nachos, 149
Native Ch'i's (nondairy cheese), 97
Native Chop Chop salad, 175
Native Foods restaurants, 6–7
Native Iced Tea, 305
Native Nachos, 149
Neato Refritos: Mexican Refried Beans, 269
nondairy cheese. *See* cheese, nondairy
noodles
    soba, 27
    udon, 30
nutritional yeast, 31
nuts
    chestnut, 19
    glazed, 282

oats, 58, 292
oils, fats, overview, 25–29
onions, caramelized, 102
Oopa Moussaka, 218–19
organic food, agriculture, 12–13
orange and cranberry relish, 93

Palm Desert Date Shake, 308
Palm Springs Wrap (Tempeh Salad), 196
pans, overview, 32–33, 36, 49
Papa's Yugoslavian Ivar, 144
pasta
    Pasta Bolognese, 240
    primavera, 241
    salads using, 180, 183
Peanut Butter Cinnamon Topping, 280
peanut sauce, 122
peas, green, soup using, 161
peas, split
    how to cook, 54–55
    soups using, 156
peas and beans, overview, 52–56

peeling squash, 163
peppers, sweet. *See also* chili peppers
    Brunoise cut, 45
    with eggplant, puréed (ivar), 144
Perestroika (Russian Salad), 177
pesto, pumpkin seed, 123
Philly Peppersteak sandwich, 194–95
pickles
    cabbage (kim chee), 148
    cucumber, 89
    daikon and umeboshi, 90
pies
    banana cream, 276
    chocolate cookie pie crust, 283
    chocolate silk pie, 283–84
    flaky crust for, 277
    pumpkin, 275
Pineapple Upside Down Cake, 288–89
pinto beans
    how to cook, 53
    refried Mexican-style, 269
plum (umeboshi), 30–31
Poltz Burrito, 201
ponzu, 109
Portobello mushrooms
    burgers, with Yugoslavian Ivar, 200
    and seitan burgers, 199
Portuguese Greens Soup (Caldo Verde), 157
Potage Saint-Germain (Whirled Peas), 161
potatoes
    breakfast, thyme-flavored, 246
    mashed, with roasted garlic, 258
    potato salad, lemon, 184
    potato salad, Russian, 177
    roasted, with lemon, 260
pots and pans, general information, 32–33, 36, 49
preparation methods, glossary of, 44–46
Pretty Pink Pickles, 90
protein, soy, 72–77
puddings. *See* desserts, sweets
Puff Pastry Pot Pies, 238
Pumpkin Plum Dressing, 108
Pumpkin Seed Pesto, 123

Quickie Banana Almond Sundae, 281
quick rice, 59
Quick Tofu Egg, 178
quinoa
    basic information, 26, 59
    Quinoa Tabouli, 189

radishes, daikon, 21
ranch dressing, 112
Rasta Pasta Primavera, 241
Ray's Good Home Blackening Spice, 101
refritos (refried beans), 269
relish, cranberry orange, 93
rice, 59–60
    coconut-flavored, 253
    fried, Japanese-style, 255
    fried, with vegetables, 254
    rice flour, 26
    rice noodles (udon), 30
    rice vinegar, 26
    steamed, Mexican-style, 256
ricotta, tofu, 98
Roasted Barley Tea, 314
Roasted Garlic Cloves, 86
Roasted Garlic Oil, 86
Roasted Garlic Mashed Potatoes, 258
Roasted Lemon Potatoes, 260
Roasted Winter Roots and Vegetables, 248
roasting technique, 46
Rocket Burger, 200
Rockin' Moroccan Marinade, 132
roll cutting technique, 46
root vegetables, roasted, 248
Russian Velvet soup, 153
Ruth's Awesome Threesome, 137
rye and rye flour, 60

safflower oil, 26
salad dressings
    Caesar, 112
    Green Goddess, 105
    lemon-garlic, 106
    Madison's, 115
    ponzu, 109

pumpkin plum, 108
ranch, 112
Thousand Island, 111
vinaigrette, balsamic, 104
vinaigrette, curry lime, 114
vinaigrette, mango lime, 107
vinaigrette, sesame orange, 110
salads
    black bean, with cornmeal dumplings, 176
    Caesar, 169
    chop chop, 175
    fattoush, 182
    with grains and seeds, 167
    Greek, 181
    jicama, 173
    lemon potato, 184
    macaroni, 183
    with pasta and salsa, 180
    quinoa tabouli, 189
    Russian beet and potato, 177
    with taco meat and salsa, 170
    tempeh, 171
    Thai-style cole slaw, 188
    tofu egg, 178
    Tuno (tuna alternative), 187
    using soy brests, 179
    Waldorf, 185
    watermelon, 186
    with wild mushrooms, 168
    yam, 174
salsas
    banana, 131
    Italian, 120
    Salsa de Chupacabra, 100
    Salsa Fresca, 121
salt
    and cooking beans, 56
    sea salt, 26–27
    sesame (gomasio), 95
Sambuca Crème, 302
Sam's Vegan Cheesecake, 285
sandwiches, wraps
    hummus, 191
    Italian, hot, 193

peppersteak, 194–95
Portobello mushroom burger with ivar, 200
seitan and black bean burritos, 201
seitan burger, barbecued, with caramelized
    onions, 203
seitan burger, with Portobello mushroom, 199
soy cream cheese with tomato and onion, 209
tacos, Korean, 206
tacos, Mexican, 205
tahini and watercress, 210
tempeh burgers, 198
tempeh salad, 196
tempeh with Caesar dressing, 197
tofu and pesto, 207–8
TuNO salad, 192
zucchini rosemary, 203
Sassy Sweet and Sour Sauce, 126
saucepans, measurements used for, 49
sauces, dipping sauces
    banana salsa, 131
    barbecue, 128
    Béchamel, 218
    curry, 117
    green tea sesame, 127
    Hollandaise, 133
    Italian salsa, 120
    jerk marinade, 130
    marinara, 118
    Moroccan marinade, 132
    peanut, 122
    ponzu, 109
    pumpkin seed pesto, 123
    sesame curry, 146
    shallot mushroom gravy, 125
    sweet and sour, 126
    tartar sauce, 129
    wild mushroom, 124
Sautéed Chard with Onions, 249
Sautéed and Grilled Brests, 77
"save the chicken." See soy brests; Chinese "Save
    the Chicken" Salad; Jerked "Save the Chicken"
scallions. See green onions
scaloppine technique, 47
scrambled tofu, 245

seasonings, spices, overview, 19–31
sea vegetables. See also specific vegetables
    agar from, 17
    general information, 27
seeds
    hemp, 23
    sesame, 27, 29
seitan
    barbecued, with caramelized onions, 203
    basic information, 27, 66–68
    basic recipe, 69–71
    burgers, with Portobello mushrooms, 199
    burritos, 201, 202
    fried rice using, 254
    Hungarian Goulash, 217
    Seitan Broth, 70
    Seitan Olé Molé, 221–22
    Stronganoff, 220
    tzimmes using, 250
sesame. See also tahini
    sesame curry dip, 146
    green tea sesame sauce, 127
    sesame oil, 27
    Sesame Orange Vinaigrette, 110
    sesame salt (gomasio), 95
    sesame seeds, 27, 29, 94
'70's Delight sandwich, 191
shakes, smoothies. See beverages
shallots
    Shallot Mushroom Gravy, 125
    slicing, 47
shortening, vegetable, 27, 49
shredding technique, 47
side dishes
    arame, 267
    artichokes, steamed, 251–52
    chard, sautéed with onions, 249
    coconut-flavored rice, 253
    corn bread, 265
    French toast, spicy, 244
    green beans with Portobello mushrooms, 257
    greens, simple recipe, 259
    hijiki, 268
    kasha varnishkas, 264

side dishes (*continued*)
    leeks with lemon, 263
    naan (East Indian onion bread), 266
    pinto beans, refried Mexican-style, 269
    potatoes, mashed with garlic, 258
    potatoes, roasted with lemon, 260
    potatoes, thyme-flavored breakfast, 246
    rice, fried Japanese-style, 255
    rice, fried vegetable, 254
    rice, steamed, Mexican-style, 256
    stuffing, cranberry and chestnut, 247
    tofu, scrambled, 244
    tzimmes, 250
    vegetables, grilled, 270
    vegetables, roasted, 248
    yams, tangerine-flavored, 261
    yams, tequila lime flavored, 262
silken style tofu, 79
Simple Deglaze, 65
Simple Marinara, 118
Simple Pleasures salad, 172
slicer, for vegetables, 36
slicing technique, 47
snacks. *See* appetizers, snacks
soba noodles, 27
Sophie's Stuffed Mushrooms, 145
soups
    asparagus, 162
    black bean, with "masa" balls, 159–60
    butternut squash with lemon grass, 163
    corn chowder, 158
    gazpacho, 154
    general tips, 151
    green pea, 161
    greens, Portuguese-style, 157
    lentil, 154
    minestrone, 164–65
    miso, 152
    root vegetables and lentils, 153
    split pea, 156
sour cream, soy, 28
Soy Amigo salad, 170
soybeans, 21, 25–30, 53–54. *See also* cheese,
    nondairy; tempeh; tofu

soy brests
    chicken fried steak, 230
    general information, 72, 76
    Mad Cowboy barbecue, 227–28
    reconstitution for, 76
    roasted, jerked, 242
    salad using, 179
    sautéed and grilled, 77
soy citrus dressing, 109
soy cream cheese
    cheesecake using, 285
    cream cheese, soy, 27–28
    "dream" cheese frosting, 273
    and tomato bagel sandwich, 209
soy milk, 28, 36
soy protein textures, general information, 72–77
soy sauce, 28
soy sour cream, 28, 285
Spanakopita, 141–42
Speedy Kim Chee, 148
spelt, spelt berries, 28, 60, 62
spices, seasonings, overview, 19–31
spinach, 141–42
split peas
    basic information, 54–55
    soups using, 156
spring onions. *See* green onions
squash, butternut, soup, 163
Steak Morocco, 232
Steamed Artichokes, 251
steaming technique, 47–48
Stroganoff Seitansky, 220
strudel, apple, 293–94
stuffing, cranberry and chestnut, 247
sucrose, 25
sugar. *See* sweetening agents
sumac, 182
Summer Grilled Vegetables, 270
sun-dried tomatoes, 29
sunflower oil, 29
sweat beans. *See* soybeans
sweating eggplant, technique for, 219
Sweet Ginger Cream, 303
Sweet Green Soybeans (Edamame), 135

Sweet and Sour Nuggets, 237
sweet and sour sauce, 126
sweet brown rice, 59
sweetening agents
    barley malt syrup, 18
    maple syrup, 24–25
    sugar, organic, 28–29

tabouli, 29, 189
Taco Meat, 74
tacos
    Korean-style, 206
    Mexican-style, 205
tahini
    basic information, 29
    nondairy cheese from, 97
    sandwiches using, 210
tamari, 29
Tangerine Yams, 261
Tanya's Tempeh Salad, 171
tapenade, 140
Tartar Sauce, 129
Tastes Like Caramel Apple, 278
Tata's Tapenade, 140
teas
    bancha, 18
    iced, 305
    roasted barley, 19, 314
teff, 29
Teflon-coated pans, 32–33
tempeh
    basic information, 29–30, 63–64
    Basic Prep, 65
    burgers, 198
    in French Love Bites, 139
    how to make, 65
    pâté recipe, 138
    pâté wrap, 196
    salad with, 171
    sautéed with peanut sauce, 150
    Tempeh Provençale, 216
    Tempeh Scaloppine with Shallot Mushroom
        Gravy, 215
    Thai-style stir-fry, 233

wrap, with Caesar dressing, 197
Tempeh Pâté, 138
Tequila Lime Yams, 262
textured soy protein, 72–77
Thai Peanut Sauce, 122
Thai Slaw, 188
Thai Sticks, 150
Thai Tempeh Stir-Fry, 233
thickening agents
    agar, 17
    arrowroot, 18
    corn starch, 20
    kuzu, 23
Thousand Island Dressing, 111
Thyme for Breakfast Potatoes, 246
Tijuana Tacos, 205
toast
    French, 244
    garlic, 87
Toasted Almond and Currant Chutney, 88
Toasted Sesame Seeds, 94
toasting technique, 48
tofu
    baked, with quinoa and yams, 223
    banana cream pie, 276
    basic information, 30, 78–80
    egg, 178
    egg salad, 178, 245
    marinade for, 80
    sandwich, with pesto, 207–8
    with spinach and Hollandaise sauce, 223
    with Thai Peanut Sauce, 236
    Tofu Feta, 99
    Tofu Ricotta, 98, 229
    Tofu Scrambler, 245
    Tofu Short Stack, 223
tomatillo, 30, 100
tomatoes, sun-dried, 28–29
tomato sauces. See sauces, dipping sauces
Totally Stacked Enchiladas, 212–13
Tuesday's Mediterranean Sandwich, 207–8
Tuno (tuna alternative)
    basic information, 30
    TuNO salad, 187

Tuno (tuna alternative) (*continued*)
    TuNO Salad Sandwich, 192
turmeric, 30
Tzimmes, 250

udon, 30
umeboshi plum
    basic information, 30–31
    in daikon pickles, 90
    salad dressings using, 108
utensils, recommended, 33–35

Vanilla Crème, 301
vegan, defined, 11
Vegan Béchamel Sauce, 218
vegetable pot pies, 238
vegetables, overview, 21–30
vegetarian lifestyle, 7–12
Vera's Voluptuous Veggie Fried Rice, 254
vinaigrettes. See salad dressings
vinegars
    apple cider, 18
    balsamic, 18
    rice, 26

wakame, 31
Waldorf salad, 185

Warm and Wild Mushroom Salad, 168
water, for cooking grains, summary table, 62
Watermelon Chill salad, 186
wheat. *See also* seitan
    bulgur, 19
    couscous, 20–21
    gluten flour, 22–23
    wheat berries, 31
    Wheat Berry Waldorf Salad, 185
Whirled Peas, 161
wild mushroom sauce, 124
wild rice, 60
Won't You Arame, Bill, 267

yams
    pudding, chestnuts, 300
    tangerine-flavored, 261
    tequila lime-flavored, 262
    yam salad, 174
yeast, nutritional, 31
Yugoslavian ivar, 144

Zen Cucumber Bites, 143
zesting technique, 48
Zucchini Rosemary Sandwich, 203